CW01498011

CONTENTS

COVER PAGE

VICTOR CARSON

A MEMOIR

This Is Not The World, I Was Promised.

DISSATISFACTION

DISSATISFACTION

This Is Not,
The World,
I Was Promised.

A MEMOIR

VICTOR CARSON

VICTOR CARSON

TITLE PAGE

DISSATISFACTION

DEDICATION

I know that my parents - Victor Owusu &
Mary Oteng Owusu- are the kindest, most
generous spirits I have ever known, and
that what is best in me I owe it to them.

AUTHOR'S NOTE

My name is Victor Carson. The fundamental fact that I have written this book you are holding is absolutely preposterous. I have not achieved anything extraordinary. My greatest accomplishments so far have been becoming a first-generation and boarding a plane—a relatively average feat. However, I have this firm belief that there will be no sane world left for me and my generation to even sieve together the elements of what we want to do with our lives as to consider making a substance out of it or getting to the pinnacle of our destinations.

This book stands as a personal backscattering and introspective analysis of this moribund world defined by unfulfilled promises, where leaders of only two decades ago pledged so much yet achieved little to nothing, and where contemporary figures navigate governance with alarming special-interest and ideological blindness. It is a memoir infused with principled observations, drawn from decades of witnessing the erosion of ideals, the advance of tyranny, and a pervasive disillusionment with those at the helm and in our neighborhoods.

I intend for this work, in the pages ahead, to be as a solemn reminder that we are warped off the course of history toward a path that demands restoration and wholehearted healing—not only of our fractured societies but of nature itself.

The "promised land" envisioned by Moses and, in our ultra-modern history, by Dr. Martin Luther King Jr., was a land seen from the mountaintop, a vision of unity, hope and prosperity that now feels perilously out of reach.

The world long revered as a powerful badge of progress and a beacon for moral stewardship now appears sabotaged. Deeply-seated modest venerations and metaphysical values completely slaughtered. Family bonds are shipwrecked. My kindest mother uncertain about the world she had conceived for her children. And the realm of leadership has too often deteriorated due to voidness of personhoods, blankly spirited for higher responsibilities, wielding sovereignty with an immaturity unbecoming of their offices.

This is not the future I was raised to believe in, nor the world our forebearers prophesied. This one is foul, dubious and diabolical. The streets are restless. My eyes burn with the anger of a honey badger. This feels like a betrayal. This is nothing like the world I was promised. Like most people, whether you live in the small towns or big cities; there must be something out there for me. Something satisfying. The substantial sacrifices and the persistent passion cannot be nonexistent. Something must happen and it must happen quickly.

I stand at a crossroad, faced with a choice to either settle for a hollow, deranged version of what might have been or to pursue, with renewed resolve, a path of integrity, progress and purity. I call on you to join forces with me. My hope is that this book will provoke meditation, calling forth a global commitment to reclaim the principles that carried the promised mappings and propel us toward a better, just, and an enthralling society.

THIS   PAGE   IS   LEFT   BLANK INTENTIONALLY

CHAPTER ONE:

PROLOGUE: THE WORLD IS BROKEN!

*"And there will be signs in sun
and moon and stars,
and upon the earth distress of
nations in perplexity
at the roaring of the sea and the
waves men fainting
with fear and with foreboding of what is
coming on the world; for the
powers of the heavens
will be shaken. And then they will see
the son of man coming in a cloud
with power and great glory.
Now when these things begin to take place,
look up and raise your heads,*

because your redemption is drawing near."
Luke 21 : 25-28

H istory is definitely unhappy and plainly unelicited. Young people and cities are occupied with vile rage, violence and despair. Nocturnal field crickets switched off their vuvuzelas at night. No one morally or epistemologically knows which side of the coin is the head or which policies to rally behind; that's should the microchip of potent balanced believe systems is still well-regulated and well-positioned and not displaced by an officious multiculturally evolved microscopic deadly viruses.

The freedom fighters used their societal licenses to embark on something else on their enemy lists and are neither reliably righteous nor trustworthy after ceremonially and cheerfully granted the pious opportunity to power by ordinary people; emancipating through the pivotal outraged mind of Abraham Lincoln. Major currencies and economies have taken administrative leaves in a civilization endowed and furnished with legion of young daring dreamers, dissatisfied dragons and draconian standards.

The President of the United States

with his mundanity walking steps skated the staircase of the Air Force One, executively surged and hijacked traffic regulations with his motorcade and civic duty through state police reinforcements and Secret Service, meticulously mounted on an early presidential debate stage in July 2024 moderated by Dana Bash and Jake Tapper of the right-wing legacy media CNN: without any fraction of a functional ideal of what the hell he was doing or where he was; left the desolate world with gringo memes, unguarded humor, roared schemers and later an iron-fist organized Sunday-school democratic coup rocketed in a single post on X formerly known as Twitter.

Educational and Research Institutional organs have prioritized meanness over intelligence, conformity over critical thinking, while sponsoring reduction of detailed meaningful coarse works and cancellations of eventful course-correct seminars. As exponentially important as a university education is, young students are dropping out as they are waking up to the new script that there will be no world left for them to accomplish the dreams, they tell themselves in the mirror or the lyrics they sing in the shower.

The South African immigrant Elon Musk and his SpaceX company recently pulled out one of the greatest technological mysteries in human history by shooting a rocket into outer space and parallel-parked it back on planet Earth. However, did not receive the Presidential Medal of Honor or appraisal due to wedlock identity politics after his public declaration support for bravery, free speech, and his pledge to join the President Donald Trump's movement that promises to 'Make America Great Again' in the midst of two assassination attempts.

Community parade grounds for commonsense are water under bridge. The ashen bones of many veterans are poisoned by youthful hypersensitivity mctrics and manipulative doses. Female athletes have unfortunately lost nearly a thousand worth of medals and modest accolades to ex-males with masculine genotypic expressions; whom after their doctor's appointments transgendered to become approved rivals, clashed against traditional women in decorated women's sporting categories and continuum.

North Korea and North Asia borderline Russia, famously known as rogue and ruthless superpowers, a bundle of nuclear foes of the West, have become tight buddies with an unendingly rekindled and sparkled romance coexisting between them. The Head of Syria is the sidekick to join the kissing party. Christ the King is perennially and courageously substituted in his own temple by mortals manufactured by his effervescent handy works and bearers of his breath of life and reconstituted by optimal psychotherapy.

The designated ambassadors graciously elected, crowned and merited to largely represent and circuit the many Israelites from the den of Pharoah in places like de Gaulle's France and the Great Britain are now the triumphant sounding boards for division, recalibrated Marxism, intellectual oppression, and terror with limited rhetoric for common ground salvation and spirited assurances that people can be good donators to grassroots civilizations.

The doomsday on the nauseating streets of Ankara and the sickening living rooms of Amsterdam consequentially projects the graveyard as a waterproof best resort for driven and yielded admirers far above the succinct people of Micronesia.

I am a hundred percent certain that, the half-life archeological excavation of the skeleton of Nelson Mandela if not eternally proven, would be magnified in optimism than an African mother who just had twins in a valley of darkness with no home to return or a young charismatic Scottish idealist who wishes to defy the odds for a second Independence Referendum.

The passenger train stations, and road marked bus stops in major cities of London and Liverpool are the newly converted and registered vicinities for thug of wars of Tobacco mainstream smoke and flying hangover vodka bottles as well as late night contaminated drools serving as host for communicable bacterial infections and fetuses of a Mexican fer-de-lance serpents. The United Nations indisputably and denotatively have less than seventeen minutes of the full ninety left to fulfill over hundred and thirty strategies compressed into seventeen incredibly sophisticated and assiduously crafted Sustainable Development Goals (SDGs) by 2030.

I have full reservation and patent skepticism that they do possess or intend to borrow a string fiber of the gallant "remontada" deterministic DNA of the vintage and glitterati football Club, Real Madrid. The UN of today can neither sponsor nor sovereignly oversee the harmonious gentle growth of tomato seeds in Belgium and Bangkok or the cargo shipments of blue jeans and semi-conductors across the South China sea without military intervention.

From South Africa to Southeast Asia, it appears that the competent Statesmen and ambitious women that came together to end World War I, World War II and the Cold War literally not figuratively succumbed with their ideas and operative playbooks fastened to their caskets. The Silent Generation and the Baby Boomers have totally obliterated the existence of that courageous powerhouse. Souls are being disenfranchised by irreverence and unsavory conversations about race and religion, color dominance and creed disorder at the dinner table, parking lots and around water cooler dispensers.

The wind cries for clemency for the breach of the Ten Commandments and for the inhuman institutional child marriage of Iranian eight-year-old girls just as they are on the verge of becoming articulated in speech making and able to cross conventional roads without parental or samaritan guidelines. The House of Commons of the United Kingdom just issued a credible license to incompetent medical practitioners who cannot defend their oath of offices to save lives by ending them on the grounds of Assisted Dying Bill forgotten the clear fact that; even not out of compassion, but the odds that laws widen in scope overtime, and the right to die may become the obligation to die.

Bloody coups have been restored this time; with unique petitions and outcry signatures from the united mass semblance of both the upperclassmen and the occupiers of the poverty threshold with no magnanimous reason of forgiveness to stand down but red-hot vengeful retribution in and around the ever-spanning great Sahara regions and the far lands of the Islamic Emirate of Afghanistan.

"*I-Am-Your-Brother's-Keeper*" is bantered and catfished to your known and broad day familiar facetime killer. Patrons and overnight protestants armed with country flags and heartfelt solidarity are reframed as drug cartels and war criminals, and are singled out, gunned down and walked upon in Jomo Kenyatta's Kingdom and Sukarno's Indonesia like Neil Amstrong walking on the moon.

The tainted hatred and the tiptoed resentment mounting up among mankind across all sectors and sailors, predominantly from the beaches of the Normandy to the Loch Lomond parks of Balloch to Bantama in the Western coast of Africa, are too terrorizing to the highest peripheral that the birds of the air no longer fly within reach as they fear not just the culmination of poisonous gases to disrupt their lungs by induced industrial fumes or being hunted down by the stones of playing kids but the smell of the sheer iniquitousness of the people and banal treachery in its enthroned form of specialization.

The household running water is not only clogged with comprehensive resistors for maximum water electrolysis but with streamlined angrier e-coli's that lurch rhinoceroses in its miniature texture. Many seniors across Europe and the "Great State" of Canada halted their automated inflows and participations to several medical appointments as they have opted to utilize whatever dime or penny they have in their coffers, even if they had safety nets, to settle their exorbitant mortgage prepayments for their kid's future, and made peace with any acquired chronic or concealed immunogenetic infections dwindling their health and crusading their mortal days to a final heist.

Broader grins on the faces of civilians and residents during grocery shopping in various supermarkets like Lidl, Tesco, Costco, and neighboring corner shops is a thing of the past as unreasonable inflation notwithstanding the reckless spending of governments, is a known and accepted pandemic like the Wuhan Coronavirus.

The episodic calm of the sixties amidst the cold war and the electric thrills of the eighties of Ronald Reagan and Jerry John Rawlings had long been replaced by a sullen emotion befitting the coming decade of shortages, defeat, doubt, and limits especially after the 2012 UN General Assembly. The intelligent ones like JFK and MLK and Alex Salmond; who were long on vision and wit were short on life and temperament.

The legacy media belongs to the Big Gun donors like Bill Gates, Bernard Arnault, and folks on the Jeffrey Epstein and Sean John Combs "Diddy" lists. Loyalist and down-to-earth mothers have given up and trashed out their own sons and daughters in bins as expected per the documentations in the great chronicles of the book of Isaiah. The incarceration confinements are now for those without deep pockets and never for the rule of law, sustenance for humanity and the safeguarding of corridors of chambers.

The Jihadists rule the Northern Hemisphere of the planet by day and the Hedonists forcibly rape young women and vulnerable girls by night in the Southern poles. This is not the world that put babies and doses of raw dopamine releasing hormone, happiness in the arms of incapable wombs through genetic engineering and decent embryonic development and restored and boosted the hopes of slaves sitting around the fire during the uncordial bedlam and sung songs of freedom in the post Apocalypse.

This is not the world that rekindled the darker ingenuity and led the commitment of Alan Turing and Steve Jobs to their unprecedented and mind-boggling heights in exponential technological growths and advancements in the twilight of a never-ever imagined undoable restricted worldview that today makes a middle-aged father living in the caves of Timbuktu to witness firsthand information about the massacre in Gaza on a broad day televised news or a talented school girl in Terhan to press play and boggy to the streams of songs of the 2023 Time Magazine Person of the Year, Taylor Swift on a YouTube channel or the world that guides a native Jamaican old woman to shop on Amazon in her own native language on a single handheld device and expect to see a decent transactional business of her purchased goods on her doorstep in couple days.

This is not the world that Mohamed Bouazizi sought out to reclaim by setting himself on fire making a fatal example of himself; never a shame, to put in the ignition for the commencement of the Arab Spring that stalled and diffused unfair leadership behaviors and unfair denizen treatments in Casablanca, Samaria and Damascus. This world has become acclimatized to seeing grassland innocent workers and oftentimes sinless penchants categorized as troubledly-flunked inescapable collateral losses especially when testing for a new military equipment in the farmsteads of Pakistan.

The environmentalists' dream to turn the world to windmills electricity power source has simultaneously turned those places to memorial parks of natural wild lives of many significant species of birds. The people that advocated for the conversion and plantation of these windmills run away from the truth that these machineries become pointless and impractical after five to ten years as they begin to rot and rust and they omit themselves from conventional conversations beckoning its effectiveness in the global space of green, clean air and affordable energy.

The fog of exhaustion after a minimum wage shift in a hub as an agent or a lab as a medic or a classroom as a math teacher or in the face of a Puerto Rican Next or Moss Bros retailer is part of the seasonal reasons behind the explanation of the incremental numbers of mental health problems across the globe. Public opinion shows little compassion to both accused criminals and elected oath-taking public officials. Some are beginning to welcome the school of thoughts that they have similar evolutionary ties and social glue track records at least in some practices and postures.

The watchers of the nineties were not wrong to imagine that justice is not only whatever the judge ate for breakfast but also whoever has enough influence and clout to plant narcotics in the lockers and desks of that particular attorney's kids at school. Wokeism changed and refurbished people brain-dead and they stopped having kids which is among the greatest blessings offered to mankind. Your uncle just died and the reactionary verdict from your colleague is that "well he the luckiest one as he gets to sorrow no more."

This is not the world that men like Thomas Jefferson and Kwame Nkrumah saw on the rock of ages: challenged the Overton Window, marshalled, sweated, and broke the colonial plague of dishonesty, pestilence, and barbaric oppression, wrote the Declaration of Independence, replaced humiliation with humanitarianism and brought mighty nations from their knees to the decision-making table just as King David made it possible for Mephibosheth.

Global fertility rates have plummeted and reduced dramatically from 5 children per woman in the 1950s to approximately 2.3 today, which is also heading toward below replacement by the 2050s. I know this because my mother had six kids. Four decades later, the women of my generation explain that having kids are not only expensive but a nightmare - a room-of-no-return. A starring flammable pot of poverty and DINKS (Double Income No Kids) hype.

We are the people of the world, and the People Make the World as Glaswegians boast and highlight on several municipal Billboards. No matter how inscrutable the surrounding may be, this is our only home until perhaps scatterbrained genius and SpaceX ingenuity open the invisible gates to the multiplanetary civilizations. In other words, that is if providence is to condone with the egregious militant secularism, and a world where fathers tuck their kids at night and pack their remnants into a box in the morning after hearing a thunderous boomerang sound of nuclear fission. As global attention is diverted elsewhere, Romania, a NATO member, has just invalidated an election over issues of disinformation.

This is the world now.

This book fundamentally offers you, the reader, the boring but eventful chance of meaningful reflection on the disillusionments, deviations and the unmet expectations in our contemporary society.

I explore the subject matter and the designer motifs of broken promises both near and far, through personal hurdles, my grandfather's societal irresolution and global debacles and an irate yearning for a better future.

My singular narration in the pages ahead to be uncovered captures the stark and deep juxtapositions between idealistic visions and harsh realities to not just edge readers to take steps back and reconsider their aspirations and the state of the
world around them, but to be boosted to slash unnecessary regulations and sweetened protocols as this is our solemn obligation as we remain steadfastly connected and ionized, bounded by more than oxygenated air in the lungs, airline tickets and umbilical cords of mothers. This is not a motivational book. Neither is it an orthodox commentary nor a story of frictional connection.

These are the current transactional trends and unbearable events happening around you and me, both. This is a call to duty and a memorandum for action to avert a bleak future like that of the Titanic, where gold bars are thrown from a sinking ship, or a pandemic where some prosper while others suffer and die or the troubling rise of disingenuous leaderships who not only ignore the struggles and simple needs of the people, they are meant to serve but also display a startling lack of respect for the sweat and sacrifices made by those who came before them.

If you agree that, in the permanence of God, the future people are as important as we are, then this eccentric book is for you.

Here are my humble strategies for my friends and neighbours:

Sail with me.
Make a can-do plan.
Snooze your iPhone.
Shut down the Freely television from any sickening and nauseating propaganda.
Young men put the console down.
If you can, play Enya in the background and,
Begin your widest and most winnable awakening journey to the mountain top.

CHAPTER TWO:

MOTHERS WITH FADING HOPE

"She opens her mouth with wisdom,
and the teaching of kindness is on her tongue.
She looks well to the ways of her household,
and does not eat the bread of idleness.
Her children rise up and call her blessed;
her husband also, and he praises her:
Many women have done excellently,
but you surpass them all."
Proverbs 31: 26-29

A s dawn breaks, the morning sun spills across the horizon, casting a soft and a golden glow that governs the world in intimacy and infinite possibilities. In that particularly transformative decade, the era of Glasnost had come to an end, the Soviet bloc dissolved, and Nelson Mandela made his final exit from Robben Island. The year 1996 was marked as a cultural watershed, heralding the release of landmark films such as Independence Day, a summer blockbuster that captivated audiences worldwide, and The English Patient, which would eventually claim the Academy Award for Best Picture.

The music landscape was equally dynamic, as grunge and hip-hop ascended to the forefront of popular culture. Artists like Alanis Morissette, Slim Busterr and the hip-hop group OutKast were making waves on the charts, while the Spice Girls emerged as a pop phenomenon, promoting themes of girl power.

This period mapped the final stretch and the closing chapter of the millennial generation, the descendants—sons, daughters and orphans of the Baby Boomers. Websites like Hotmail and Yahoo had already made undulations and kinesiology. Amazon started to gain traction, introducing uncommon talking points and new discussions that would pave the way for the digital era. At the time, no one, not even Jeff Bezos, could have anticipated that Amazon would eventually grow into a trillion-dollar company nearly three decades later. The debut of the inaugural version of Internet Explorer significantly shaped the trajectory of the evolving digital landscape.

My mother will also be preparing to checkout from the St. Elizabeth Catholic Hospital. Her accommodation in the maternity ward was bathed in a soft, fluorescent glow and moisture. Her heart racing with a mixture of joy and exhaustion after welcoming the fourth born of four gentlemen after eight long years. She laid alone in her bed. Her life's treasured partner and most trusted lover my dad, was not around. Though she understood that she would need him. And by her side was the only place, he would have loved to be, like he had graciously been previously. My paternal grandfather had passed away leaving my dad in a whirlwind of emotions.

The morning before; both my parents were set to travel but they had to go their separate ways. My dad to his hometown to bury his father, and my mom to the hospital to have a baby for my father.

In the moments after the birth, there was nothing dreamlike about the experience; instead, the profound gravity of motherhood settled once more upon her shoulders. She had traversed this journey before, wandered these familiar halls countless times. She required no external validation; she was the experience itself. Like Deborah who stood by her wisdom and leadership, guiding Israel to victory in battle as corresponded in the Book of Judges, she knew deep down that she was more than qualified to be a mother again. One child was a challenge, two even more so—but she had four.

She had once hoped for a daughter to complement her array and lineup of boys one day, however she found no discontent in receiving another son. Her steadfast faith, much like that of the woman with the issue of blood, will ultimately be rewarded. She would go on to have another son, followed by the long-awaited arrival of a precious daughter—my younger sister.

However, that particular day at the hospital, something extraordinary unfolded. As a wave of love enveloped her, and the pat of congratulatory hands were thrown at her back, beneath the comforting warmth stirred a subtle yet persistent anxiety, gnawing at her. It was not because my father was absent, nor because her long-departed mother couldn't witness the blessings of her children; it was something deeper, an unease that she couldn't quite place. She struggled to understand the overwhelming pain and sense of uncertainty that radiated through her body, particularly in her limbs, as if her very being were consumed by an unexplainable tension.

The obstetricians' attention was drawn to her condition, but out of their professionalism, they simply advised her to rest, offering no explanation of the severity of the situation. They couldn't bring themselves to tell her that the woman who went into the hospital whole would return broken. My father, caught between two worlds, could not stay for the funeral. He had to be in two places at once. In desperation, he petitioned his siblings, explaining that he had to be at the hospital. The first call he received informed him that his wife had delivered a healthy baby boy; the second was urgent, calling him away immediately. Imagine the turmoil he must have felt—the darkness of thoughts that could have wounded him deeply.

As for me, I am not sure I was ready to face the loss, nor to bear the unthinkable avoirdupois of being known as the child who caused her mother's death. I would be given a nickname — Stranger —part of it stemmed from the cultural African tradition of naming children not in the hospital like mostly seen in European movies, but only once they've arrived home. The other designated part was the kid who brought grace into the twilight of their world, arriving with such intensity and grandeur that even the formidable strength of my mother's legs could not endure the density of it.

The following morning, the cool air of the night waited and greeted her as my father opened the door to the outside world for her. The stars twinkled overhead, a revelation of hope to the chaos in her mind. She was wandered to the pending cab, the unfamiliar contours grounding her. Sitting on a wheelchair, she closed her eyes, allowing the silence to flood over her. She garnered and thought about simple tasks: getting out of bed, moving around the house, even holding Stranger comfortably would become monumental challenges. The last part; that is not written in her archival curated manuscripts of raising kids.

Dad helped her park herself, the Stranger and her wheelchair into the lurking cab. There would be no home health aides to come and go, assisting with the basics, as there aren't enough wages for such secondaries. As the weeks passed, mom spirits begun to lift, shaken but resolute. She was not confined to her chair or the floor. Her mind was active as always, filled with unrestricted hope and blazing determination. Her hands could mount on walls, as she slides through the living room without any help. She still kept and sustained regulations and bye laws at home for the other three boys when dad was off to work or on errands.

My mom never for once considered herself as a bystander in her own life and that of her family's life but the ideological co-planner together with my dad. She would weave through the adventures of gaining consciousness and sense of upward mobility again in her upper limbs and near-staminode shafts and soon will begin to test the pedals of her feet by running and doing her own internal sit downs under the military set of instructions and patronage of my dad.

The bittersweet juncture of maternal obstetric palsy was over. She obtained restorative grace from God and small disciplinary actions, which advanced her strength, transforming what once felt like a burden into a journey of amour, victory and resilience.

As Hillary Clinton, First Lady of the United States during her husband Bill Clinton's presidency, focused on various initiatives, particularly in the areas of health care, education, and women's rights; my mother, was finally freed from any temporary life-threatening disability and renewed biologically. She was enchanted to re-adopt fulltime enterprise of passionate fondness and confidential bilateral friendship with my dad. The pair were prepared to limelight on the provision of healthcare insurance coverage for the boys and Stranger, and food security at the table at all times. The strands of hierarchical arrangements of the ladder of admissible good deeds and inadmissible ugly deeds for the boys,

Stranger (after released from breastfeeding) and their neighborly friends were aligned like that of the renowned Abraham Maslow's postulates of needs and actualization.

In a quaint and underdeveloped suburban community; everyone was familiar with the owner of the chickens and goats roaming freely, streetlights were scarce, traffic lights inexistent, even in far places that had traffic lights, the red light was more of a suggestion than a lawful command. Red meant should I stop? The majority of the indigenous population lacked formal education; it was unsurprising that two out of three adults remained uneducated but witty in their own fashion. Despite their profound connection to the land, they firmly believed that enrolling your children in public or private schools held little significance. To them, the most valuable classrooms were those found beneath the open sky—the vast expanse of farmland that surrounded them.

I grew up in a family of eight, mom and dad inclusive, life was a tropical storm of activity, noise, and trouble. Our home, a small boys' quartered house was filled with the humor, tactics, and worrisome of my siblings —three older brothers, two younger siblings, and me, the Stranger. There was a cataclysmic sequence of lessons and every day brought its own set of challenges and struggles. I always had reservations and never agreed with the restrictions set by the head of the chambers and oftentimes found myself on the edge of the cliff of knowledge and a cluster of unanswered questions in and around why there is no running water in the house or why some people are tagged as the royals and worthy leaders of the society.

There was neither an indoor plumbing nor a dinner table at the house. Plates were neatly arranged on the floor, whenever food was ready to be served. Occasionally, fowl droppings laid nearby, a detail that was mostly overlooked, but not me. I couldn't focus on my meal with that distraction, so I always covered it with sand—brushing it away would only spread the smell. This was not envisioned as hardship for me, it became a part of our daily routine and miraculously saw it as just the worm in horseradish, the world was horseradish. The trips to the nearby bushes were never just about necessity; they were filled with playful escapades and shared stories.

My younger brother, Bright, is my unknowingly truest childhood friend. Though I have many one-way friends. Some of them don't even know that I exist. Infact a larger portion of my great friends are dead. Some of my great dead friends were either in my grandmothers' or Fyodor Dostoevsky's dispensation. On the other side of the spectrum, most of these one-way friends of mine, I suppose, I have never had any digital conversations or traded ravens or tweets or exchanged letters which outmoded now but was a crucial element of communication then. From creche to college to Chinatown, London; they were all over the iconic spots, renowned landmarks and improbable minefields of the world, all of whom had minds of their own and set of illustrations to get by.

This cabal of companions I imitated impetuously. That, I dismissed after careful evaluations. The third I objected and defended especially when they were not in the ballroom of interventional dialogues. They are still my friends and I always cherished even more so. Bright and I traveled the bush each rising day by navigating and meandering through thick grass and encountering the occasional insects—we learned to embrace it. We invented a game of spotting different fruit plants and critters along the way, turning the journey into an adventure. "Look! A Scorpion!" his eyes wide with wonder and fear, and we would speed off through the forest jumping over logs and covered pits like Chuck Norris and the Delta Force and literally reciting the beats of that movie out loud.

Dad is popularly known for many fundamental essentials. The presiding elder of a charismatic church on Sundays and among his co-workers as the most prolific, productive and resourceful person. He is nicknamed as Wang-Yu. He worked twice as hard and engaged in many community seminars. He would divert to agricultural work after the closure of the only Timber Company in the community. This industry outsourced finished products to South Africa and Switzerland.

Due to ineffective leadership and sluggish regulatory frameworks, corruption has flourished unchecked, prematurely resulting in numerous disadvantaged households, broken marriages, and a rise in social vices and poverty. He tends to his modest plot of land with dedication and thought us the importance of firm handshakes with his somehow calloused hands from years of labor.

Raising six kids with no college education for the providence of a civil servant job was no small feat. The couple often faced insurmountable challenges—crop failures, limited resources, and the daily struggles of providing for a large family. Dad approached every obstacle with unwavering determination. He believed that hard work and resilience would pave the way for his children's future. I watched and learned from my father's behavior.

In the face of difficulties, unlike Pol Pot of Cambodia and the infamous Khmer Rouge whose regime was marked by extreme violence, forced labor, and widespread famine, my dad do not only showcase composed congressional leadership and constitutional character before his family, friends and fireworks but also ethical soundness through the teachings of absolute fate and hopeful stories in and around the prospects of better-days-ahead. The beacon of grace and elegance in the stories he always shared with us when we were young, carried the boldness and I was deeply moved and profoundly stirred by the ecstasies and goodness of the promised land.

Dumfries House, a distinguished gem of 18th-century Georgian architecture, stands gracefully in the heart of Ayrshire's serene countryside, just beyond the urban bustle of Glasgow. The facility was designed by the masterful Robert Adam, the house exudes an ambience of quiet grandeur, its stately façade of pale stone and classical columns evoking both elegance and timelessness. Set amidst meticulously landscaped gardens, the house is framed by an expansive parkland, where the gentle rise and fall of the land seem to echo the graceful lines of its architecture. Here, nature and human ingenuity are perfectly intertwined, creating a space that invites both contemplation and awe. As I meander through the rolling lawns of Dumfries House with my dear friend, Duchess, the estate reveals its deeper charms— its tranquility a balm to the senses.

The path beneath our feet is lined with towering trees, their leaves rustling in the breeze, while the air is tinged with the scent of blooming flowers their vibrant hues dotting the landscape like brushstrokes of color. The sense of history is palpable, like a living painting. The light of the afternoon sun casts a golden glow over the scene, softening the edges of the historic house and illuminating the lush, green expanse before us.

The air is rich with the scent of flowers, The park feels alive—alive not only with the energy of nature, but with the presence of families enjoying the space. A group of mothers, some with prams, gently push their little ones along the paths, their soft murmurs of conversation blending with the rustle of the leaves in the breeze. The prams, a reminder of a simpler time, move quietly across the lawn, each mother's gaze lovingly fixed on her child.

I saw couple fathers in summer shirts lift their children onto their shoulders, the little ones squealing in delight as they take in the world from a higher vantage point. Their faces, wrapped with joy, reflecting the love and care of those who have come to enjoy a peaceful afternoon in this serene corner of the world. Children, meanwhile, were scattered across the park, their unregulated laughter rose in waves as they engaged in the pure joy of play. Some were spotted chasing one another across the lawns, others form small groups, sharing games and toys, their youthful energy infusing the space with a lightheartedness that perfectly complements the peaceful surroundings. Among them were a group of young children accompanied by their female teachers, who had come for an excursion.

The teachers watch with gentle eyes, guiding the children's curiosity as they explore the park's nooks and crannies, learning not just from the environment around them but from one another. Amidst this idyllic scene, the park's resident squirrels, ever playful and opportunistic, added a touch of mischief to the atmosphere. One in particular catches my attention—quick and nimble, it darted across the grass, making off with a biscuit from a nearby picnic blanket before anyone could react. It abused the eighth of the Ten commandments. It was theft, while amusing, was a testament to the audacity of nature's creatures, who move freely in this protected environment. I beamed at the sight, but I couldn't help but think of how different the situation might be in other parts of the world.

Were we in Africa, such behavior might be met with a more pragmatic approach. There, survival often dictates the terms of engagement between humans and animals.A squirrel's theft might have led to swift consequences, and perhaps even the surrounding forest would have be threatened if it posed a challenge to human life or resources.

The Dumfries House operates under a different set of principles—those of compassion and preservation. Here, and like many other parks across the country, under the watchful eye of the Animal Rights Commission, these squirrels are not only protected but celebrated as part of the ecosystem that surrounds the estate. The playful theft of a biscuit is tolerated, even cherished, as a part of the natural life that thrives in this space.

Along the lines of these scenes, I was reminded of a story from my neighborhood about a hysterical hardworking man that found a black cobra, its gleaming scales catching the light in the corner of his kitchen. He phoned the animal welfare department for professional help and instead of offering guidance on how to stay safe or assuring the dispatch of trained handlers, the agent blurted out, *"Sir, just find a stick and smash its head!"* It was super hilarious and super hapless.

As I continued my walk, soaking in the serenity of the estate, I was struck by the deeper wisdom embedded in this scene of everyday life. The rawness of children, carefree and unburdened, echoed across the lawns, a reminder of the boundless potential that exists in youth. But this joy was not born in a vacuum; it is made possible through the unwavering love and sacrifice of mothers who, day in and day out, invest not just in their children's happiness but in their future. These mothers, with their quiet strength and immeasurable devotion, are the foundation upon which the next generation builds.

They give their children not only the material things they may have lacked but, more importantly, the intangible gifts of hope, resilience, and the belief in something greater. Fathers, too, are present, standing as guardians, guiding their little ones from broken branches and wetlands. The security, sustenance and stability they provide are not just the foundation of a family, but the bedrock upon which a better, more compassionate future is built. It is through their naturalism that society's greatest treasures—our children—are allowed to flourish. I was prompted that this may not be so for long especially in the Western hemisphere.

Motherhood is not only overlooked or increasingly challenged; its London Bridged in the world. It specialized intestines and deep connective tissues of — unconditional love and selfless giving — are spilled onto the floor after been attacked by a machine gun. Across the continents from the facade of Tunis to the alpines of Turin to the great city of New York, Times Square it is been looked down upon and extinguished. This wonderful stapler as it's been known for many years to have transcended mere social fabrications and mutations, as a recognizably profound institution almost timeless state of being that reveals the deepest layers of human existence, aspiration, and endurance is now categorically unhinged, unbalanced and under siege.

In the animal kingdom, there is no good or evil, no future and definitely no conservative logic beyond, "if I do Alpha, I will get Charlie", however the taxonomical mother of ducks embodies a gentler vigilant presence in the natural world. The mother of the duck, the hen; has enormous patience and resilience, gliding effortlessly across the water, her movements graceful and purposeful, like a guardian of the ripples and reeds. With soft, muted plumage—often in shades of earthy brown, cream, or gray—she is dressed to camouflage into her surroundings, a quiet protector who doesn't seek the spotlight or morality but commands respect all the same. The eyes are sharp, watching not just her brood but the world around her.

Each chick follows in a perfect line, trusting her implicitly as she leads them across ponds, through grasses, and along muddy banks. Her quacks are low and instructive, almost meditative, each sound a reminder that she is there, guiding them safely. In the duck world, she is a fierce nurturer, always scanning for dangers, be it a hungry hawk above or a sneaky fox lurking by the water's edge. In the Ghanaian Language, that attitude is rewarded with an emphatic name called, "*obaatanpa*" meaning caring mother.

The mother of ducks has a philosophy of freedom and independence for her young ones.

She nudges her ducklings forward, allowing them moments of time and space to explore, within and beyond the circus, yet they always circle back, instinctively tethered to her by an invisible thread of trust and security.

She understands the need for her ducklings to test the water, literally and figuratively, teaching them the strength and skill they'll need to one day paddle off on their own. Mind you she does this without any instinctive metric of primetime convocation. She has been doing this from primitive generations to our time of insistent Artificial intelligence and Robotics.

Young women used to dream and prioritize about fateful marriages and to have their territorial fair share on the mothering island. The current empirical verifications automatically dictate that this is now a tightrope as humanity mothership is on the verge of being completely obliterated from the social fabric by the disarray of tenderness and fondness for a new breed of civilizations.

The philosophical declension in the last decade is a complicated phenomenon shaped by shifting societal values, economic pressures, and a deep rethinking of individual identity. Once viewed as a life role imbued with existential meaning, has gradually been redefined and, in various shapes and sequels, de-emphasized and de-industrialized by modernity's focus on superficial things: like self-aggrandizement, equality, and autonomation.

This shift is not about mothers or the children they raise, but rather about the lines of weariness and newfound wisdom etched in the minds of thousands of females about unraveled dreams, unfinished works of art, emotional contingencies, structural incompetencies and other marginal significance placed upon the back of the role itself in contemporary cultures. We once had mothers that understood the meaning and the jurisdictional functions of sacrifice and aimful determination of the inherent purpose of having kids and the ever-engaging optimist look in a mother's face who could not provide breakfast to the children in the shawlands of Secondi or sylvan of San Francisco but remained cocksure that with conviction and a few market roams, there shall be abundance of vegetables and vitamins in the evening, which they did.

That substance of craving and hankering is dimmed, fraught and reduced to an unknown deputized Antartica. People have forgotten that any culture that does not hold the infant dies. The straight narrow path that it's never an end but a relationship, a connection and an unbreakable intergenerational bond of a legacy. How can we elucidate to individuals such as Mother Teresa and Eleanor Roosevelt that their confidence in modernity's capacity to uphold their fundamental values, safeguard cultural heritage, and reinforce the family unit has been eroded by the incremental influence of global media, urbanization, and the gradual encroachment of pervasive appeal of modern lifestyles, all of which have redefined these social structures?

In the late 1900s, my mother articulated a vision rooted in the belief that specific ideologies and teachings given to children could lead to extraordinary, even unimaginable, results. Meanwhile, the natural biological processes of human development are being increasingly influenced and altered by the use of puberty blockers and controversial birth control practices, marking a significant shift in societal childbearing and upbringing conventions.

I will learn in biology class the findings of Aristotle as he contested the premise famously that the family and the state as deeply interconnected entities, drawing a compelling analogy to the relationship between a body and its organs. He proposed that "the state serves as the overarching structure that supports individual families, much like the body sustains the functioning of its organs. Just as a hand or foot cannot survive without the body, families rely on the stability and governance provided by the state to thrive." This interdependent relationship emphasizes the crucial role of the state—in this context, acting as the mother—in nurturing and ensuring the well-being of its constituent units.

Asian cultures are known widely oftentimes as deeply rooted in collectivist values, where family and community bonds are held in high esteem is fundamentally and speedily depreciating. The conceptualization is factored in self-serving egotistical demonization where eternal treasure is no longer found and is identically replicating in the decline of populations in countries like Japan. This is not a matter of wishes but facts.

The relative symbiosis of a good country is centralized in the plausible Jewish proverb that, "God could not be everywhere, and therefore he made mothers." is adversely looked down upon, subverted and portrayed as mean battles. This new trend is serious and poses too many challenges in every corner of the world.

The genetic assimilation of this great establishment needs to be redefined on the primal level. The Missing In Action of important traits during the probabilities of the internet and digitalization were not to be a benchmark to leave this remarkable spirit behind. This is not about pro-choice or pro-life but the appropriation and promotion of sober analysis of frightening onlooking evolutionary scenarios, and the instinct to lead with resolve and a historically known identity.

There are few things in our cavillations and compartmentalization that do not need to be podcasted through the optical niche of divisiveness and public opinionated people. This is a resolute function and has evolutionarily been marketed in a modest way and emerged as the successful venture. History and relevance have to be running the show and not the elocutionary of politicking and protracting everything into the arena of progressivism and socialism. You can be a mother and raise kids and strategically fulfill your life's goals and help shape that of your kids. That is true, which sets and kept civilizations before us free but that basic nonnegotiable practice is at war.

Celina Caesar run a research firm including raising two kids and later ran for office in the world of Canadian politics where people were silenced to speak during questioning periods. You can become a parliamentarian secretary or a plastic surgeon with serious and packed schedules for patients and the public and still excel because humans are multifaceted and wired to process fundamentals without any gaps and attain a satisfactory outcome of benevolence. Two-year-olds would be smearing the contents of their diapers on the walls of the living room and the screens of the television sets and tablet devices and even consider refrigerating themselves in the fridge if it wasn't for the presence of competent mothers.

This is far from the world; I was promised by my mother. This is deeply troubling and incredibly dangerous as the smallest particle of grains with warranted rottenness will overlap the entire editorial pagoda of society. Mom advises me to go right whenever everyone around me goes left. She wants her children to be different—uniquely themselves, authentic, and unafraid of standing apart—do something beautiful and brave and not be trotted out. She corrects gently with reason and common sense, not to mold us to fit in but to help us find the courage to embrace what sets us genuinely apart with substance and threshold. Her guidance isn't about conformity, regardless of the importance of age or position.

She reminds me think before I step outside, to decide definitively on some terms, to act with integrity at all times, and listen to my own heart even when it means walking alone.

In this communal approach, she did not simply raise me; she raised me and my siblings with a sense of fairness and without indulgence, shaping us into individuals who would venture into the world with the courage and distinction to be authentic—whether contributing to something grandly revolutionary or a humbler trust fund. And perhaps the most remarkable part of her guidance is that her children, though different from each other in not just age, interests and choices but also in ethics and temperament and also from those around us, and will always carry the similarly quiet undiminished wisdom.

She instilled in us: to be fully fledged emperors with clothes on, culturally civic and not unimportantly provocative, belligerently organized and not teeteringly undecisive, competently brave and not absurdly parasitized by modern day woke mind virus. She constantly ascends the idea that, we may have left the garden but we should always remember where we are coming from; including the building blocks of why we would be doing whatever mission we chose to do. She advices us to be unapologetic and ideationally sound and never tolerate being sidelined by psychological tokenism, institutional depression, undefeated systemic racism, and the grooming dictatorship of wokeism.

The reentering of the vital executive function of motherhood is the psychedelic revelations of the existence of civilizations. The notion that modern logics have abandoned the truth about mothering, found on a number of occasions dismissing it as an inconvenient social construct, currently is what is in front of us, and it offers absurd impacts on first and foremost the nuclear family, then the long rope of communities, and the world at large.

This restoration doesn't mean idealizing or glamorizing motherhood but rather walking the line with upward aim with the elements of vision and reorientations to straddle the frenetic being of order and chaos which maximally generates an environment where motherhood is respected, supported, and celebrated in its true complexity. Career and productivity metrics in this known reductionist preceptive world we will reside in today, with all sorts of transformations and attractiveness, should not affect and obliviate the rhetoric of nurturing and the metabolism of kids on sacred grounds.

Children need an idealistic childhood and the paradigm of this great ecosystem has theoretically profound consequence to automatically shape the matter in which the psyche of every individual modifies itself in habits and society corpus. What's happening not only to Afghan mothers and Iranian underaged girls but also across the Western climate where the schedule now is only focused on the most illegal of illegal things and have thrown water on these things seemed to have worked.

The confusing era of the 1970s between where the effects worn off and women started doing coke, aborting 6months old of pregnancy, had make up on, big hairs as the music sucked in this moment is unforgivable and the connection of sounds and fossil records make all of us responsible.

How radically different would our world have been if Roman mythology, with goddesses like Juno, the goddess of marriage and childbirth, and Maia, the goddess of fertility, had symbolized aspects of motherhood as real, human experiences rather than divine or mythological ideals? What if they had embraced the sentimentalized, glorified notions of motherhood perpetuated by their immense influence, instead of acknowledging the more complex and often obscured realities of motherhood in ancient Rome?

It is preposterous to suggest that the struggles and achievements of mortal mothers, who were seldom depicted heroically or celebrated in Roman literature or art, could ever be regarded as exemplary or manageable in the context of modern democratic ideals. The notion that their experiences, rarely the focus of narrative or cultural acclaim, would somehow be elevated after the advent of democratic programs and the passage of rights—an assertion rooted in ignorance—undermines the complexity and historical context of maternal roles.

Many women today find themselves in a state of discontent, as the institutions and roles that once defined them have been tragically distorted into something far removed from their true essence. The younger generation of women, particularly, has shifted focus from nurturing motherhood to chasing after transient symbols of status, like the latest designer bags.

This chapter of the book has been the

enlightenment to the catastrophic mushroom semen powdering this enormous pine corn of the woman's identity. This modern-day cancerous California fire is not only destroying important women duties and God-given-role as the bearer of future warriors and the sustainer of incredible virtues and values largely seen through the lens of their massive contributions to the world through fertility rituals, family lineage, and societal continuity but has reframed these responsibilities as burdens.

This is the harsh reality of our world today. I cannot help but question: what will become of us just half a decade from now, as these misguided priorities continue to deepen their hold? This current state of our world should not be a model for broader communities to worship. This is comparably a hedonist anarchy influencing the balance of our minds. And we must fight, fight, fight!

Follow the manifestations of the underlining ministry of the next chapters to fathom the intrinsic cardinal benefits of becoming aware of the non-conformist and unstructured despondency of your neighborhood and the far radical integration of your social organization.

CHAPTER THREE:

THE UNITED NATIONS: NOW A TOP HOLIDAY DESTINATION

"Woe to you, O land, when your king is a child,
And your princes feast in the morning!
Happy are you, O land,
when your king is a son of nobility,
and your princes feast at the proper time,
for strength, and not for drunkenness!"
Ecclesiastes 10:16-17

I n 1945, the Nazi regime crumbled, and the world's leaders grappled with the consequences of a catastrophic war. The Nazi defeat was met with relief, but it left Europe devastated and the world reeling from the horrors of the Holocaust, as well as the immense loss of life and destruction. These events laid the groundwork for a new era of global cooperation, and the involvement of what would become the United Nations was crucial to shaping the post-war order. The United Nations was founded with high hopes, born from the ashes of World War II to protect and unite a fractured and a degenerated world.

In October of that year, Manchester, England, hosted the remarkable 5th Pan-African Congress. It was a landmark event that brought together African and Caribbean leaders to discuss independence and strategies for anti-colonial movements. Ghanaian nationalists like Kwame Nkrumah and George Padmore participated, making critical connections with other African leaders and activists.

The conference emphasized that African nations must achieve immediate independence from colonial rule and encouraged participants to return to their countries to mobilize and lead independence efforts. Kwame Nkrumah was especially influenced by the congress and returned to the Gold Coast inspired to take on a leadership role in the independence movement.

Common sense was at bay, and the Abrahamic blessings of the Fathers of Nations were unfolding rapidly. There was an inherent fight against Dawin's characterization of humans and human's reproductions as the selfish genes, and was proven as wrong. Men began to think about the mutigenerational taxation and the patterns of freedom and liberty. The United Nations was literally becoming a living testament of the great rhetorical Declarations of Independence drafter by Thomas Jefferson in 1776 which postulated that, "we hold these truths to be self-evident, that all men are created equal, that they are endowed by their Creator with certain unalienable Rights, that among these are Life, Liberty and the pursuit of Happiness." Leaders and citizens alike saw the UN as a beacon for peace, a place where countries could resolve conflicts, foster cooperation, and ensure human rights globally. In its early years, the UN made significant strides, helping to rebuild post-war societies, combat hunger, and foster cooperation. But over time, something began to change.

As time passed, the world grew more complex, weak leaders were born and were tolerated to participate on the highest stages of reformations and editorial illustrations of the world.

In 2009, I began to see the world differently. The beginning of enlightenment and habit realization were scooped out of my immediate surroundings even though my frontal lobe particularly will hiatus, until just over a thousand days ago to become fully developed, as known by neuroscience. The dusty paths, long walks to school without the installation of any school buses to wheel us, the mango trees that me and my crew; Bright and two other boys, hunted on the weekends, the hard chuckling of the village elders sitting under the reserved baobab tree playing cards, the irregularities of the electricity power generation, popularized anew as "dumsor" meaning "switching the lights on and off" countless times a day: all of these held new layers of gunshot and horsepower meanings I hadn't noticed before.

I was only twelve, but that year, something inside me stirred, a curiosity that pinched like an itch I couldn't quite scratch. I became a young boy in some form with incredible coping mechanisms. I cognitively memorized and recited the definitions of subjects like digestion, frictional force etc, in primary school integrated science classes. I was introduced to the readership of greater extension of books by my dad. I overcame natural phobias like chatting to girls, public speaking and adopted both defensive and offensive mechanisms against inescapable bullying.

I obtained conceptual learning and the primacy of the highest quality of better speaking intonation and incredible inclination of poems and reggae storms. AI was a far-fetched mirage if not a wandered hallucination. Outdoor games were replaced by the godfather social media which was declared to eternally stay. Academic progress was well plotted without any bitterness. My handwriting became more legible and refined than that of many renowned doctors and radiologists worldwide.

I was exposed in the spirit of the contextual affairs of the world. I prayed for the salvation of my soul and the subcortical motivations for my long-term gratification. I began to regulate stupid pleasurable things in the moment that would not compromise my destiny. During this moment in history, the man, the myth, the legend, Michael Jackson was experiencing some sort of a deteriorating mental health. I was espoused to a practical degree of self-assessment and the assimilation of the biblical library of Adam and Eve to subdue the world.

I was freed from childhood unawareness and idiocy. Everything seemed to be in its proper place and the whole structure to operate and excel in was in a state of harmony and synchrony.

My father purchased a colored television which was a rare opportunity to get by and a crypto level of asset at the time. Long bamboo stick was utilized to mount an antenna as a practical solution regularly employed in rural or low-resource settings to enhance TV signal reception. The antenna's angle and orientation were adjusted by tilting or rotating the bamboo pole, which was essential for aligning with the satellite's direction or broadcast tower. The effectiveness of this setup depended on the quality of the antenna and the proximity to the signal source.

Aside from watching major UN executive speeches and programs, often alongside my dad, and enjoying nighttime movies and nuanced news with the rest of my family, the inauguration of Barack Obama, the first Black president of the United States, stood out as a vivid memory I held in conspicuous and striking detail. It was a moment I would revisit time and again on YouTube, serving as both a catalyst and a testament to the possibility of achieving success on the highest pedestal.

Dad managed to set up a small generator and a projected screen, making it possible for everyone especially the young ones to witness history. What stuck out for me wasn't the promise of change, the hope of unity, and the idea that a Black man could lead the most powerful nation in the world regardless of either he followed his policy transcripts or not. It was for two fundamental things; his improbable story and for the decline of systemic racism.

The notion that the grandson of an undocumented cook, once of lower rank in the British Army, could rise to become a president in any country—let alone the United States—was nothing short of miraculous.

Moreover, the imaginary vision that a black man from Kenya could not only ascend to the zenith of the most racially dystopian and entrenched system in human history, a network that gave rise to the tragic deaths of Emmett Till in the 1950s, and more recently, George Floyd, Breonna Taylor and Ahmaud Arbery in the 2020s, but run it meant that systemic racism was over and done. It was positive for the internet generation and affirmed that the sacrifices of figures like Martin Luther King Jr. were not in vain.

The UN organization itself, however, grew bigger, ironically slower and more entangled in its own systems. Bureaucracy bloomed, and decisions have been intertwined and wired in drawn-out debates instead of swift, decisive actions. The national interests for the African people of Botswana collides with the imminent floods of the Spaniards of Valencia in Spain. Favoritism committees all working with their own mandates, budgets, and policies.

This very structure designed by brave men to address a wide range of issues—human rights, health, education, environment has since become an obstacle to regional and global effectiveness. The unimportant behavior of agencies often duplicate efforts, complicating clear communication and stalling progress is killing more lives.

Redundancies in reporting requirements, interdepartmental friction, and convoluted hierarchies lead to delays that weaken the organization's ability to respond swiftly and decisively to global crises. Nations found themselves with new economic and environmental concerns, facing crises the founders of the establishment had never envisioned. The Security Council, tasked with maintaining global peace and security, is arguably the UN's most powerful body, but it is also the most constrained by political power dynamics.

The five permanent members (P5)—the United States, Russia, China, the United Kingdom, and France—each hold veto power, allowing any one of them to block actions, even if they have global support.

This concentration of power creates a geopolitical deadlock, where strategic interests of the P5 regularly prevent the UN from acting on critical issues. Economic conflicts in Syria and Slovakia, and the Russia-Ukraine war, and the ages of combat in the Middle East exemplify how the United Nations' hands are tied when just one powerful nation disagrees or is involved. The veto system effectively neutralizes the proclivity and capability to take unified, decisive action, compromising its foundational purpose of maintaining global peace.

This has caused widespread cynicism and eroded public trust, with many viewing the Global Coalition as a stage for superpower dominance rather than a body dedicated to peace. The internal accountability mechanisms of this infrastructure are weak and unchecked. Reports of mismanagement and even allegations of corruption and abuse within the unit's missions and agencies go unaddressed due to the complex internal processes needed to investigate and resolve these issues. Additionally, there is limited transparency in how funding is allocated and spent, particularly in large programs run by agencies such as the World Health Organization (WHO) and the United Nations Development Programme (UNDP).

This roost of accountability does not only diminish and blur the substance of effectiveness of programs but also damages the elemental credibility for growth and development especially within the democratically developing nations in Africa and Asia. Donor countries control the trajectories of how funds are issued and which buyouts are monetized.

The public are often left in the dark about how resources are used, leading to skepticism and hesitance to provide funding. Ultimately, this undermines the capacity of the global alliance to execute meaningful, large-scale initiatives to treat malaria and cholera in the sub-Sahara regions. As originally intended to be a cooperative effort supported by its member nations, its operational budget and initiatives rely heavily on donations from a few wealthy countries and individuals.

This dependency compromises the United Nations neutrality, as donor nations often expect influence in return. Furthermore, funding constraints mean that many subcommittee agencies within the organization operate on thin budgets, frequently shifting priorities to meet donor interests, which have diverged from the original goals of the setup. The reliance on donor funding has led to short-term, piecemeal solutions rather than sustainable, long-term interventions. For example, the climate programs are frequently underfunded or interrupted due to inconsistent donations, limiting the international community's role in fighting climate change and reducing its ability to address pressing environmental issues effectively.

Part of United Nations' fundamental missions are upholding international laws and norms, particularly in areas like human rights and territorial sovereignty. However, its mechanisms to enforce these laws are inconsistent and often politically motivated. For instance, human rights violations by powerful countries or their allies are frequently overlooked due to diplomatic pressures, while smaller nations may face sanctions or condemnations more readily. This selective enforcement weakens the framework's legitimacy and emboldens violators of international law, as there are limited consequences.

Inaction in places like Myanmar, for example, highlights the discrepancy between the world body's rhetoric and its willingness to act, diminishing the necessary authority and fostering a perception that it only enforces rules selectively.

Calls for reform within the United Nations have existed for decades, however significant institutional change remains elusive. The internal culture is heavily resistant to reform, often defaulting to the status quo and the overtone window to preserve established power structures. Efforts to reform the Security Council, increase transparency, or streamline bureaucracy face entrenched opposition from those who benefit from the existing structure. The fact is that without ideological reform, this global assembly becomes increasingly irrelevant as it struggles to keep up with contemporary planetary issues. Many of its processes and structures were designed for the world of the 1940s and fail to meet the demands of the modern era, such as digital misinformation, cyber warfare, and rapid climate change.

The Millennium Development Goals (MDGs), which were established in 2000 by Kofi Annan, the former Secretary-General of the United Nations, aimed at addressing global challenges with deadlines notably 2015, did a marvelous job. His administration pioneered the agenda to eight basic reasons: from eradicating extreme poverty and hunger to achieving universal primary education to the promotion of gender equality and women empowerment to the reduction of child mortality to improving maternal health to ensuring environmental sustainability to the development of global partnership and to combat HIV/AIDS, malaria, and other diseases. They performed an exceptionally remarkable and unprecedented job.

I am not just commending a fellow Ghanaian.

I witnessed the drastic changes during his tenure. I saw the massive changes in basic thing: mosquito nets were provided to African schools; little girls were encouraged to partake in healthy lifestyles. Actions were executed toward vulnerable regions and the integrity of commonsense was upheld so that the famine of the 1930s in Kyiv, Ukraine and 1980s in Abuja, Nigeria would forever remain ancient history.

I had all of these plans committed to memory during my final year of high school. I can confidently say that not a single person alive—be they Harvard students, English professors, or even the very organizers of the current goals—could list all 17 Sustainable Development Goals (SDGs) along with their 30 objectives without resorting to the internet. This isn't a matter of memory prowess; it speaks to the growing disengagement and lack of genuine interest in the institution itself.

The emergence of COVID-19 as a global pandemic in late 2019 and early 2020 was a complex event and was influenced by various factors, including political, social, and scientific dynamics. This escaped the global antennae and the sharpness of the United Nations from its inception and identification in Wuhan, China. This thing, renamed by President Trump during his first stint in the White House as the "China virus", took away serious businesses and lives with it.

The whistleblower's report revealing that Chinese authorities failed to promptly inform the World Health Organization (WHO) about the emergence of a pneumonia-like illness was a clear case of incompetence and deception, aimed at concealing their errors to maintain their authority. Moreover, there has been a disturbing amount of misleading information and misinformation from prominent figures in the medical community, such as Dr. Anthony Fauci, who is now facing scrutiny for his contradictory statements during such a critical period in history.

◆◆◆

I remember where I was when this caricature struck by reconnecting with my past and how the world was generally unprepared for a pandemic of this magnitude and scale, despite warnings from experts and previous outbreaks (e.g., SARS, MERS, Ebola). I was a final-year first-generation university student at a preoccupied Kwame Nkrumah University of Science and Technology, in Africa, the motherland of mankind and a continent that has long been an enigma to its people and the rest of the world. It was supposed to be my last semester of eight, and I could almost taste the freedom that awaited me and my friends beyond exams and the appreciation of the beauty and grace of the journey itself.

I was majoring in Biological Sciences, with expectations of one day working in an environmental conservatory or medical law firms or an entrepreneur as the non-occupational programs in most African universities prepare students to become a jack of many traits with a pool of Graduate School options to ponder and cherry-pick from. My academical and social campus life had been a long series of exams, faith seeking evangelical programs, relevant projects, community services, debate, and late-night study sessions. These were fueled mostly by five minutes cooker noodles popularly known as "indomie" and

Auntie Muni's waakye.

The finish line was in sight. The semester had started as usual, with midway examination protruding in the rearview with his foot on the accelerator. It was my last hurdle, and I'd invested countless nights studying, desperate to finish strong. But as the weekend wore off, whispers began circulating on campus.

Some virus had emerged in China—a strange illness causing fevers, coughs, and difficulty breathing. Unlike most of my colleagues that barely paid attention at first; I paid considerable amount of time to global news due to my backdrop interests in fundamental books, revisionist history, geopolitical debates, Pan Africanism and American epistemologies. But by mid-February, the virus had spread far beyond China, and mutters turned to alarm. Social media was flooded with updates on the virus that now had a name: COVID-19.

Cases were spreading across borders like a cultural diffusion of the famous MAGA souvenir hats. Soon two sufferers were reported at the doorstep in my country. The school was abuzz with rumors of potential closures by the Sunday morning. I watched with a mixture of dread and disbelief.

This was the most crucial and pivotal semester of my college life, yet everything felt like it was spinning out of my consciousness. On the brisk evening of the Sunday, I sat immersed in my studies, I was suddenly interrupted by a chorus of jubilant shouts, reverberating like the roar of the lion of Judah over Mount Olympus, followed by the loud rustle and susurrations of the night and the Howling Wolves of fireworks.

The celebrations seemed to come from near and far—hostels and housemates reveling together. Intrigued, I decided to investigate, and I noticed that the university administration issued a green sheet through email and other official student communication channels on social media: exams had been postponed until further notice, and all students were instructed to vacate the campus and return to their homes immediately.

Alone in my hostel room, I dropped dead-flat on my bed. The stare at the ceiling gripped me with immersed silence with void meanings that would be reverberated into deeply significant connotations. Everything I'd been building toward, the numerous injustices I had endured, the smaller insistent victories I had gathered, the excess pain and discomfort that I had suffered for being a grinder, the culmination of years of hard work; were now indefinitely suspended. The inconsistencies of a possible online studies, exams and a possible online graduation for final years, the first of its kind, dawned on me. It came with its own temperature in a country of unstable electricity and power supply.

I made a firm decision to remain on campus for the basic amenities, knowing I could depend on the generator, as there was no such backup at home in case of a power outage. I felt as though I were stranded on Mars, alone with my thoughts—unruly hair, eBooks at my disposal, and whatever was left in the fridge. The constant phone calls from home provided some connection, but there were no other humans in sight. As days turned into weeks and months, I came to realize I wasn't just a solitary occupant in a room, or the only person in a hostel meant for over 200 students. I was the only living being in the entire vicinity during the devastating lockdowns, trapped in an almost sealed-off world, surrounded by an overwhelming sense of trepidation and uncertainty.

Many countries had underfunded their public health systems, and global health infrastructures were insufficient to manage a rapidly spreading virus. Institutional coordination loopholes and gray matter areas of putting sauce on the safety mechanisms of the world was trashed. The famous World Health Organization's ability to formulate a global response was hampered by the sheer wizardry of the publication of clear communication and collaboration among countries. Immaterial and immoral political tensions, including those between the United States and China, affected the WHO's effectiveness, credibility and processes. It was the beginning for many people to witness the firsthand ignorance of globalization and the pitfall of humanities interconnectedness of the world through travel and trade facilitated the rapid spread of COVID-19 as people moved across borders, the virus spread before countries could implement effective travel restrictions or quarantine measures.

Seeing the asymptomatic spread of this case and its stories unfold on the screens of telecommunication devices home and abroad was hysterical. The rapid development of vaccines was a remarkable scientific achievement, but equitable distribution remained a significant challenge. Wealthier countries secured most vaccine supplies, leaving lower-income countries vulnerable despite Initiatives like COVAX which aimed to ensure equitable vaccine access, but logistical and financial barriers hindered efforts to provide vaccines to all countries.

Given the relevance of education, the world has consistently worked to improve it at least in theory— with notable successes and smeared failures. In 1800 as the transatlantic slave trade began to decline as European countries, especially Britain, officially abolished the practice by legislation and absolutely substituted it with direct colonial control and resource extraction, nearly ninety percent of the world's population was illiterate, brain dead and imbeciles in Britain and America, most people couldn't read, write or calculate. Today, more than sixty percent of the world's adults are literate and understand basic algebra.

The paradox of the MDGs of Kofi Annan were somehow particularly boastful in closing education gaps by getting people to the dormitories and behind school desks. The goals which promised to get all children into primary school, with a specific focus on girls, who are often left behind in indigenous places like the Muslim communities and Africa hit organizational walls like bureaucratic inertia, power imbalances, funding dependencies, inconsistent enforcement, which made it utterly impossible. This highlights the need for structural and cultural shifts if the alliance is to fulfill its mission effectively in the 21st century.

The global unit has no meaningful reforms and continue to exist as a symbolic entity rather than a practical force for real change. Powerful institution as it is meant to be has lost sight of their purpose and has entangled in their own mechanisms, turn up big for General Assemblies and no real team work is shown, only for Ukraine's head of State to show up and ask for money to pay their bills and buy expensive cars for his wife.

The same principles that guided the creation of the United Nations, shaped by the vision of those who signed its founding documents and viewed it through the lens of diplomacy, have faltered over time. As a result, new blocs of institutional alliances have emerged, such as BRICS, founded in 2006, which has seen an increasing number of African leaders looking to join South Africa. The G7, G20, and AUKUS are all examples of entities that operate independently of the UN, pursuing alternative paths for global governance. President Kagame of Rwanda, after securing the nation from the threat of another genocide and restoring stability, has held onto power for more than two decades, setting expectations for the United Nations that diverge from its traditional role. Antonio Guterres, a seasoned diplomat and former Prime Minister of Portugal, took office with a pragmatic understanding of the UN's shortcomings, yet his tenure is likely to be remembered as one of the unluckiest in the organization's history, particularly in terms of humanitarian leadership.

In a world where the failures of globalist ambitions have led to chaos, drone supremacy has supplanted nuclear dominance as the ultimate symbol of power. Meanwhile, the Taliban has imposed a metaphorical Berlin Wall, which has isolated women and curbing even their ability to engage in everyday conversations. Simultaneously, *TIME* magazine enthusiastically promotes a redefined notion of "having it all," now equating fulfillment with the absence of children—a stark reflection of a shifting global perspective.

In 2024, a number of African nations have witnessed a resurgence of military coups, continuing a disturbing trend observed in recent years. In July 2023, Niger underwent a military takeover, sparking regional tensions as neighboring Burkina Faso and Mali expressed their support for Niger's junta in the face of potential intervention by the Economic Community of West African States (ECOWAS). This wave of coups highlights the growing instability in the Sahel region, where ineffective United Nations policies have revived the once-forgotten conflicts. Amid rising economic hardships, security concerns, and governance failures, many citizens now prefer military-led regimes over what they see as fractured leadership and ineffective democratic systems.

The United Nations, followed closely by the Pope, is often the quickest to condemn unconstitutional changes in government, issuing swift statements that resonate globally. Yet, no tangible actions or effective sanctions follow, with the blame routinely deflected onto structural, political, or operational challenges. These declarations are disseminated across multiple languages, amplified by AI technologies, and then quietly fade into obscurity. No reforms. No meaningful change. No enduring stability. Just empty gestures, smokescreens, and rhetoric floating in the ether. How did we come to believe, even for a moment, that a body of unelected officials—many in the twilight of their cognitive sharpness—could steer the world toward meaningful progress for future generations? The very institution once heralded for championing free speech and liberation now appears aligned with powerful interests and far-left agendas, working to suppress dissenting platforms advocating open dialogue. How did this erosion of ideals occur?

The Abraham Accords, signed in September 2020 amid the global upheaval of the COVID-19 pandemic, represented a groundbreaking moment in Middle Eastern diplomacy. These accords formalized diplomatic and economic relations between Israel, the United Arab Emirates (UAE), and Bahrain, later expanding to include Morocco and Sudan. For some, the agreements symbolized a rare blessing— a beacon of hope in a world overshadowed by despair and loss. Finally, a blessing in disguise in a world seemingly teetering on the brink, some believed that the two nations signed the agreement with a vision to halt the descent into a landscape of graveyards and mass burials. These historic accords were facilitated by then-President Donald Trump during his first term, marking a pivotal effort toward fostering peace and stability in a troubled era.

As of this writing, he is widely regarded as the frontrunner in the race for the 2024 U.S. presidential elections, vying for a second term. His competition includes the formidable Democratic establishment and Vice President Kamala Harris, often referred to by Gad Sadd as the "Lobotomized Cackler." His prior term had seen ambitious plans aimed at fostering cooperation, stability, and prosperity between Bibi Netanyahu's Jerusalem and the refugee camp of Jabalia. However, the departure of Donald Trump from office marked the end of those initiatives.

This morning, like every morning, I woke up to the sound of alarms—both real and figurative. Sometimes it's a phone call, pulling me from my sleep and reminding me that the world is always moving. The second thing I noticed, after morning thanksgiving prayer was that, the persistent Syrian war and other global unrest had seized the headlines.

There were several rising tensions and murmurs of an impending third world war casting an ominous pall over daily life. As a young adult, each day dawns with a mixture of curiosity and trepidation. If allowed, it has the power to paint my carefully cultivated yet fragile sense of stability with strokes of ambiguity and unease.

I can't help but ponder the subconscious toll this will take on even younger generations—those as young as twelve—who have with unrestricted access to the internet and social media. They wake up each day to the harrowing realities of our world. From images of stray bullets lodged in the bodies of senior citizens in Judea and Samaria, to the heart-wrenching visuals of a teenager, brimming with potential, tragically shot in the mouth on the streets of Maputo, Mozambique, the exposure to such unrelenting violence shapes their perception of humanity and the world they are inheriting.

From the county offices to the central aurora avenue of from the desolate no-man's-land of the Central African Republic to the sprawling mainlands of Central Asia, let it never be said that the generation of my fathers, alongside the distant mothers of Millennials and Gen Z, chose to abandon security and stability. Let it not be recorded that they replaced these vital pillars with brutality and fatality, forsaking the very places their children would come to know as home and sanctuary.

Today, the United Nations is populated by ineffective and disenfranchised individuals who have failed to unite for the betterment of the world. This represents a clear and undeniable failure of humanity's most fundamental purpose: to leave the world in a better state than we found it. Instead, we are plagued by fragmented ideas that prevent meaningful progress, stifling basic human connections and failing to shield vulnerable communities from the dangers that threaten them.

The reluctance to embrace systemic change could also be portrayed psychologically through

Sigmund Freud's notion of the *repetition compulsion*, a drive to repeat past behaviors. Their failure to engage younger voices and focus on future-centered policies may be viewed as a post-apocalyptic signal of *presentism*, a bias that values immediate concerns over long-term consequences. This short-sighted approach mirrors political philosopher Thomas Hobbes' argument that institutions, like individuals, often act in self-preservation rather than in the interest of future security.

CHAPTER FOUR:

RABBI FIRED FROM HIS HOUSE

"In the beginning was the word
and the word was with God
and the word was God."
John 1:1

S unday mornings, as inscribed by my dad meant dressing for church left a deep imprint on my heart and memory. Each of us would kickstart with a sense of ritual and anticipation. The week's usual rhythm giving way to something special and extraordinary. Dad gathers and dedicatedly irons the clothes chosen by us, as he believes in the sense of choice and the power of decision. In the atmosphere of reverence, calmness, and Bob Marley songs in high pitch, he lip-sings and dances his brevity and regrets away throughout the entire ironing section. The ambience was something more than just putting on nice clothes—it was an act of honoring the day, a small outward expression of inward respect for the Christian faith and a sense of fulfilment for depressed faces and wretched bodies.

I could argue that I was just like any other five-year-old who was dragged to the temple in Africa or Ku Fung in China by their guardians or parents. The Bible and other great books were the focal point of discussions and not Critical Race Theory as witnessed in recent times in some of the big economies of the world.

My parents never exceeded the middle-income threshold, yet they have always believed

—and continue to believe—in the profound value of giving. For them, generosity was not merely about receiving blessings or grace in return, but about the intrinsic joy that comes from freely sharing. They understood that acts of kindness, given without attachment, can leave lasting impressions on others, igniting in the adrenaline and sense of fulfillment that has the power to dissolve any roots of anxiety, dispel negativity and witch-hunting yolks.

Mom's words, *"God loves you, and I love you more,"* at the end of each phone call, cut through any sealed walls of resistance. They were more than a simple statement; they were a grounding force, a reminder that no matter what had transpired during the week, compassion remained unwavering. It is always delivered in her calm, steadfast voice, those words become a constant source of reassurance—a comfort my siblings and I carry with us throughout the day.

For a young adult, these formal routines and doses of optimism and the iconic dance of President Trump at the end of his rallies particularly in Pittsburg, Pennsylvania on the eve of election are invisible threads that weave a sense of belonging and faith into the fabric of everyday life and that all is not shipwrecked, providing both a sense of stability and a subtle nudge toward something beyond the acts themselves. These small, repeated moments have become foundational memories, a part of what faith, family, and community mean—concepts that are always remembered, and often passed on, from one generation to the next.

We would make our way to a strange wilderness. A partially completed building which stood in a stumbled area, with rotten windows, no doors, and a fractured clock that works twice in a day and night. The plastic seats were dust-covered and stripes of bamboo served as the mighty pillars of the building. This semi-habitable space, under the radar of quantity surveyors and construction will be made ready to host us literally by selfless members that take the lead to brush the remnants of cement droppings, broken nails and unused tissues.

Driven by the teachings of the widow's offering that Jesus demonstrated to his disciples in the Bible or the ethos of Tesco's timeless slogan, 'Every Little Helps,' (no, there is no Tesco in Africa), the local members contribute what they can—small, meaningful acts that steadily build toward a greater goal. This ongoing project gradually takes shape and have been made possible by the grappling desire of common people with regular decent jobs, (most of them jobless) to manufacture and play a constituted role in getting a place for divination on earth.

The people are armed to get not just a structure but an altar where voices will rise in beckoning worship like it does at Ledgowan Tenants Hall. A community center, which will emerge as the source of all creation and renewal, will be intertwined with uplifting songs of worship, offering a profound connection that soothes and harmonizes the nervous system. A building that will echo the power and pomp that radiates almost like when Bishop Ahmed Conteh of Canterbury, from the Pentecost International Worship Centre in Glasgow, Scotland, or my kid sister Gladys, (popularly known as Ohemaa on social media) steps onto the stage, to fill the space with a presence both transformative and deeply moving.

A significant time will be scaled for the local priest to admonish the psychological consequences of the biblical stories, transcended notions of distilled salvation, immense polytheistic understanding of the return of Christ, the punishments of civil disobedience and the visible wonders of substitutionary grace. Generations would gather there, some with severe human conditions that can be found on the surface or beneath the scratched surface of their appearance; all believing in something greater than themselves. In reverence, manifolded in the pathological originator of the force of nature, a supreme being of Genesis and Revelation, the Enuma Elish.

This ideal lurks deeply inside the opening lines of my exploration of religion and its intense danger and paternal courage that enables me to overcome any evolutionary conventional spirit of the unknown. The structural economic utility of trust that got betrayed in the Garden of Eden and default instillations of a practical righteous mythologies of sacrifice held in the metaphysical perspective in the particular exhibitionism portrayed by Abraham, have been the definitive actualization that underlined many legislative orders in void and chaotic communities. The declaration of the cosmos energy in contemporary world is up against the forces of the dark and deep state of Bohemia occults evil forest.

Christianity has been experiencing a decline in adherence, particularly in Western countries. From Emmanuel Macron's France, formerly known as the Roman Gaul, which hosted the arrival of the earliest evangelists and missionaries shortly after the death of Christ, with early congregations likely established by Roman citizens and converted soldiers, traders, and penchants to the Canadian islands where Protestantism begun to spread, particularly Anglicanism, during the indefatigable colonial rule of the British people, marshalled through the Church of England and other relevant State support.

In Africa and a few segments of Southeast Asia; disturbing natural elements like: unregulated famines, disorienting diseases, xenophobic wars, boomerang earthquakes, generational poverty, and misogynist propagandized governments make their burdened indigenous people want to reach to the sculptures, paintings, and architectural designs of Michelangelo Buonarroti, the greatest artists of the Renaissance, renowned for his talents and courage.

Nations begun to rebuild after Adolf Hitler was defeated in the WWII and led to the formation of two separate German States in 1949: West Germany (Federal Republic of Germany) and East Germany (German Democratic Republic).

West Germany became a key player in the Western bloc, aligning with NATO and adopting a market economy, while East Germany fell under Soviet influence, implementing a communist regime.

The Berlin Wall, erected in 1961 was a symbol of this division, physically and ideologically dividing the two nations until reunification in 1990. Washington emerged as a superpower of the world with a significant influence on global politics, economics, and culture. London established the National Health Service (NHS) and other welfare state measures aimed at addressing social inequalities exacerbated by the war.

Moscow expanded its territory, installing communist governments in Poland, Hungary,

Czechoslovakia, and other countries, which led to increased tensions with the West. Huge decline in religious observance and institutional authority was adhered. The devastation of the war, including the Holocaust and the moral crises it raised, led many to question traditional faith and the existence of sound mannerism. Militant secular ideologies gained traction and momentum, with a shift toward radical rationalism, Sodom and Gomorrah humanism, and an emphasis on science and conscious autonomy. Churches have then seen and still are witnessing a reduction in attendance including committed leaders and faith builders themselves. The younger generations are increasingly identifying as agnostic or atheist in a world of inescapable modernization.

The rise of television evangelism and megachurches were supposed to create in some streams, new forms of worship to support emphasized interpersonal experience and coordinated emotional engagement among people of various backgrounds. However, they crashed into walls of world leaders across Europe and America who preferred otherwise.

As Billy Graham became prominent, advocating for a "Christian World" and sensible public relations, the Prime Minister of the UK from 1964 to 1970 and again from 1974 to 1976, Harold Wilson's government, was busy advocating an iron dome of socialism and finally played a significant role in advancing gay rights. The Sexual Offences Act 1967 decriminalized homosexual acts in private between consenting adults in England and Wales, marking a major milestone in the soar of modernly higher numbers in LGBTQ+ rights. Bill Clinton became recognized for his "Don't Ask, Don't Tell" (DADT) in 1993, which allowed gay individuals to serve in the military of the United States of America. Angela Merkel will legalize same-sex marriage before leaving office in 2021.

This chapter is a not a singular case that the acceptance of gay rights on the national and global level is the reason for the promises of the church to be in the mud, it is only a fraction of this tumultuous period in the history of mankind. The origination and the promotion of the Ten Commandments in the great Book of Exodus, coupled with the revolutionary engagements of Moses' spiels catalyzed the kinetic chain reaction which brought Rome to its knees and steered the earthly significant foundations not just in religious context but in the broader philosophical, ethical implications, and the conceptualization of human behavior; is at the crossroads.

Globalists with their encrypted non-Christendom woke crusade, having reframed the Christian practices as outmoded by orchestrating an outcome, have pushed Christianity out of the door of a Fast and Furious vehicle driven by Paul William Walker and had been run-over by Mark Sinclair.

The last two decades have opened the gates for this absurdity conversion and the declaration of the Easter Sunday as Transgender Day of Visibility by the Biden White House made it worse. Sports campaigns are now another paperback coliseum to mock and slam the manipulative imprints on Rabbi as the rest of the world became heavily troubled and agitated at the Opening Ceremony for Paris Olympic Games 2024.

The Last Supper established by Jesus Christ as the Eucharist, and constitutes the new covenant rooted in service, grace, and remembrance through the act of breaking bread and drinking wine, to foster unity and strength, was ambushed and stage-scorned. All faiths including Muslims, non-Christians, and digital You Tubers erupted against this sheer cowardice and ferocious televised deeds.

The transitions of raw fire and distilled water to the curation of the internet and nanotechnology, have mobilized the world to new projections and historical dynast, however not so much can be said of the church. Information can travel to anywhere around the world in micro seconds. Doctors now have more clinical trainings and machines and research details to heal, save and prolong the lives of patients unlike the past. Medical and pharmaceutical intervention have made it possible for people to have good lives and forgo guinea worm to its genocidal extinction.

People no longer have total belief in the Apostolic rhetoric of many Men of God occupying the treaties and harbors of West Virginia or West Indies. Healings from Hepatitis B or infertile wombs or systolic blood pressure are scientifically disproven. Psychology and clinical psychologists have rolled the red carpets for spiritual mental health. People now bow to the idea that the best practical course of action to have a meaningful, self-fulfilling destined life is to get to a room, get a cup of coffee and converse your life through with of some unspecified lonely gray woman paraded as a therapist, who magically has all the answers to your questions of your decaying household in hands.

Therapy is and have been a structured process in which vulnerable individuals work with a trained mental health professional to address any laser of psychological meltdown or traumatized emotional triangulation or concealed behavioral challenges. It is magnificently great, but it is not and will never be a surrogate for prayer. The Central Intelligence Agency (C.I.A) prayed during the cold war. Millions of people across the globe took to the streets and interceded for global renewal for the planet during the Covid-19.

The efficacies and the effectiveness of today's dominant materials is to provide updated services to the scriptural faith, rather than relieving it of its essential role, which has bound civilizations together since the dawn of time. The reliance on manmade things like antibiotics and seat belts should not make it possible for people to wonder if truly all things were made perfect from the beginning as read in the Hebrew scripture.

Today, many people of the gospel and the bearers of the Armor of God are malnourished, lazy and its extremely pathetic. They have abolished the fundamentalism and conservatism. They have allowed themselves to be silenced. Most of them are cognitively blank in their frontal lobes. They are grown adults with infant brains. As the world grew, their knowledge in the heavenly 'word' stayed the same. They have shallow discoveries as they have not increased in wisdom and stamina in reasoning and purity. They have no comeback missionary plan. They are the modern-day losers. There is cancer and vindictiveness amongst themselves.

Daniel was the smartest and formidable person in his network. Joseph was the most important candidate to forge the Egyptian establishment. The arrogant designs of the elite who disdain our values, beliefs and traditions seem to be winning. The congregational numbers keep plummeting in person and across broadcasting networks. Rabbi cries for resurgence against corrupt, entrenched bureaucracy in his home. I can imagine how hopeless the Son of Man has become in these turbulent times.

Aristocrats make derogatory and scatological references and incompetent remarks about the temple. The Savior has been turned to a socialist. The limbs of the victory horse are striped in chains and stabbed in a world of nihilism. The kids in schools are raised in hate oppressive drudgery instead of humility and moral values. Puberty blockers is the new flex for retarded mothers. Formal presidential aspirant Kamala Harris roared at a group of diverse people in America for celebrating Christmas, a commemorated day, the birth date of Jesus Christ. Sound priests are censored and restricted from teaching the gospel in Iran and Pakistan without any plausible shame.

In Glasgow, the place I call home, the churches herein, like many across Scotland, seemed to be tapering off—its vitality dimming, and its community dwindling and mostly filled with international students from Africa, Asia and the Middle East. These identities of personhood do not just go to church out of obligation as some do. The majorities also do so for the primacy of the facts that these places are not only a graceful call to duty for civility but also run countless assistance programs for food stampers, accommodation seekers, and also sense of belongness for washed travelers and students.

I have seen the hope in people's eyes after they realize that they are not alone and the church has a place for them and this is worth-preserving, a flicker of light even if faint or nonexistent. The church is not that place anymore as contemporary scholarship has envisioned. Newbies now do not believe in the resurrection of Christ or the inherent good in people, but they have turned to other spots like the night clubs and gym societies for this mere basic help, which often aren't transactional. The church now has turned their back on folks they ponder and categorize as extremists or had faltered a rule.

In the combat zone, captains and colleagues shine in the ethos and creed that highlights the importance in the solemn dignity of the injunction that says that, "no man should be left behind." You might wonder how big this is; this goes beyond either the soldier is dead, alive, or transplanted. This statement covers and includes those whose limbs are missing in action, nerves shattered by explosion, lungs poisoned by gases, prisoners of wars, heart decimated, even traitors. They keep the solemnity of the numbers. They cherish those ideas.

David in the biblical chorography was always alert, mindful of the dangers that could arise in an instant. He knew each sheep by sight and took his responsibility as their protector seriously. Whether it was a lamb grazing near the edge of a ravine or a sheep lingering too close to the forest's shadowy edge, David kept them all in his view. After gathering the flock into a small valley as the Bible teaches us, where they would be less likely to wander. Apostle David carefully built a protective barrier of stones and thorns around them. He positioned himself at the valley's entrance, knowing that predators would have to pass him to reach the sheep. Even while attending to his father's call, David kept his thoughts with the sheep. He frequently looked over his shoulder, ready to spring to their defense if needed.

Today, the church is the reverse of David's story. Blasphemy and bigotry are at the behest of it. People turn their back on each other while they roll up their fake sleeves and bad breathes for services. They downcast and outcast the outlaw. They mount up misanthropic and divisive hedges around them. No outlier is allowed to knock on their disentranced doors, only those who look like 'them', sound like "us" or whose last name is familiar. They banish people with immediate effects. They release those with roles and relevance from their volunteerism and servitude.

The people of today's contemporary churches lambast and broadcast the flaw. These disdainful courses of act are not only executed by just some august old church goers who are now hold offices because they are neighborly with the parking lot and grasslands, or some heavenly mandated preacher who recites the scripture by heart but a mixture of both the youth and the gray.

These lifestyles are carried out on both local and national level of these denominations. Everyone you know or knows you; including your loved ones, game center foes, people who only exist in the background of your life, the market places, the kids playing grounds, even the bulls of the farm, and the spiders in the cracks and crevices of that vicinity, develop a sense of urgency and attention to detail about a person's stigmatization and scandalization. They turn their back on each other. They turn friends against each other. They reinforce others to leave friends behind. They decimate the veracious family bonds. Venerable fathers and mothers are encouraged to forbade their children.

These are bad practices executed by bad people in masks in the house of the Lord. These office holders have experiences, but they are "bad experiences" as President Donald Trump uttered during his Presidential Debate in 2016 alongside the democratic nominee. They are people possessed with low-energy witchcraftism. They have come to steal, kill and destroy. They have not only lost touch with reality, they have also lost touch with the properly based scripture. I have witnessed firsthand a case of these immoral and uncharted territorial practices played out twelve months ago in certain traditional setting of the great UK.

Jack a vibrant, 5ft8 tall gentleman with a cleared eye, easy smile and a well-kempt beard has this particular church woven into the fabric of his everyday life. He was raised in this church and had been an integral member together with his family, since his days of childhood, and an electric instrumentalist. Under certain extraordinary conditions, he took a seed with his unofficial girlfriend and found himself at odds with his faith community. Among others, the church leaders took a strict view, believing his situation was a first-degree unforgivable sin that brought shame and reproach to the congregation.

Congregational indictments would be filed against him. They summoned him for a hot seat meeting, where he was informed that, due to the nature of his actions, he was no longer welcome to participate in church activities, serve as a youth mentor, or even attend services. They were unyielding in their belief that his actions had tainted the sanctity of the community. He was escorted out. The rejection hit Jack hard. The church was his spiritual anchor, his source of support, guidance, and now he felt completely abandoned. He had no other friends outside the temple. He tried to reach out to friends within the church, but many turned away, fearing they would be judged for associating with him. Left with a profound sense of isolation and guilt, begun to feel hopeless, wondering if he could ever find his way back to the acceptance and belonging, he once knew.

In July 2023, the international political arena was super active and engaging. NATO held a major summit in Vilnius, Lithuania, where member countries discussed the possibility of Ukraine's future membership, cooperation etc. and negotiated Sweden's accession to the alliance. The unspeakable Russia-Africa summit took place in St. Petersburg, with a focus on strengthening Russia's ties with African nations amidst the global impacts of the Russia-Ukraine conflict. India launched its Chandrayaan-3 mission to the moon, aiming to join the select group of nations capable of a successful lunar landing. The Women's World Cup kicked off in Australia and New Zealand, marking an expansion in the number of competing teams and drawing international attention.

Historic flooding in the northeastern United States, especially in Vermont, due to torrential rains, and record-breaking wildfires in Canada that burned vast areas in British Columbia. Climate crises further compounded issues across continents, particularly in the horn of Africa, where extreme drought left millions facing severe food insecurity and malnutrition. Commonsense efforts to combat climate change saw and enveloped committed African nations advocating for climate adaptation funding at COP27, hosted in Egypt. This happened a decade later, after the Egyptian murmurs had experienced a major upheaval when the military deposed and denounced the reigns of President Mohamed Morsi in 2013, sparking widespread protests and violence across the pyramids and papyrus of their Black Land.

The Summer Nights at the Bandstand festival returned to Kelvingrove Park for the ninth year with the twelve nights of live music from Gabrielle, Bananarama and others in the city of Glasgow, the second largest city and most oriented after Edinburgh, home of the First Minister of Scotland. Businesses, both the state-run bodies and the free markets, and residents were gearing up to welcome the world to the city the following week, with the imminent arrival of a world-first cycling event. I was thrilled to be at the exact place where history was happening, as this marked the first time, nearly a decade, particularly post-pandemic, Scotland had hosted such a global event. It set a new standard by combining multiple cycling disciplines into a single championship format, creating a historic "super worlds" event.

Mathieu van der Poel's victory in the men's road race, powered through a challenging 271.1 km course from Edinburgh to Glasgow, winning himself and his hardworking, the coveted rainbow jersey. Lotte Kopecky of Belgium took gold in the women's road race, triumphing over a grueling city circuit through Glasgow with steep climbs and demanding twists and turns. I could hear the blade slap of numerous helicopters circling overhead, loaded with photographers, journalists, and officials dedicated to accountability and transparency. These choppers hover high and steady, outfitted with powerful lenses and equipment to capture every detail from the ground. Photographers document the unfolding events from various angles, ensuring nothing but the truth was captured and shared with the public.

It was an amazing display of art as I watched this unfold along with many observers; the ones who left their homes, polished for the occasion and those who stood momentarily because they were drawn by the nearby crowd ovation and acclamation. I could conjure up how effectual and fruitful their presence served as a cue that eyes were on the ground and from above, pushing for responsible actions and honest reporting. From natural disasters and conflict zones to public protests and high-stakes political events, I was nudged in memory the pure commitment these air machines represent to oversight, bearing witness to events with precision as they happen and not just ensuring a historical record for all to see through bulletins and gazettes for the following day but also the lengths society goes to for transparency and fairness in the modern world.

Several uniformed accountability groups were on board at vanguard standpoints, scrutinizing the situations around with a critical and evaluative eye. British police officers and a few international ones were in their reflective green and orange jackets and patrolled the main and adjoining streets, not with forceful authority, but with an unwavering fidelity to peace and ensured that civilians felt safe, heard, and protected. I saw the delivering riders, the repeatedly —overlooked backbone of urban society, remained steady as they navigated the city streets on their electric bikes working to deliver food, parcels, and necessities to the people, regardless of the world outside. With the atmosphere thronged with camaraderie and impatience, the usual punctuality of the Glasgow Central train station became secondary as I exited among everyone out of the carriages onto the tracks and platforms wanting to grab a front row spot by the roadside.

The usual buzz of routine commuters was replaced with the sound of chants, flags waving, and sometimes even impromptu performances of team anthems: that was one of the few moments you would see a Ranger fanatic and a Celtic idealogue jumping together. The second closest is when the two giants fix bump and root together to support any other team playing particularly a football match against The Three Lions of England's national team and sometimes even in whatever sports in may be. In such surreal nanosecond, Central and Queen Street stations as known by the natives aren't just transit hubs; they become temporary community spaces, where, shared passions bridge strangers from different walks of life.

Nearby bars and eating places like Blue Lagoon at the north entrance and Nando's at the west took on an even more intense transformation. You can see the lights dim a little lower, the televisions turn brighter, and the energy in the air becomes thick with nervous excitement. These bars, usually the heart of social life in cities, become packed to the brim with fans. The clink of glasses blends with the loud laughter and shouting of obtuseness, each hoping for a victory. Whether it's a local pub or a trendy cocktail bar, these spaces become temporary sanctuaries for people to either drown their nerves or celebrate their team's success. It was beyond any impression.

Grappling to bear the magnetic pull of

shame and rejection, Jack sank into the lower forces of depression. His thoughts grew darker, and he found himself questioning the value of his own life. He began to think that maybe he didn't deserve forgiveness, that maybe his community's judgment was final. The pain and loneliness became almost unbearable, and he felt trapped with no way to move forward. I was the last person of contact. I run into Jack unscheduled. The randomness of it is farther from comprehension. We had a little unplanned conversation. It was about college, Artificial Intelligence and his sister. It was great! The image of a man walking with his son on his shoulders, heading toward a place where he plans to end his life, however haunting and tragic symbolism it may be, did not cross my mind.

It painted a picture of despair so profound that even the innocent joy a child might bring, illustrated by the son on his shoulders, could not break the man's inner turmoil. The child is unaware of the fate that looms, and the man carries him, not just physically but emotionally, burdened by a weight heavier than what his shoulders can bear, and unburdened by what was to follow. I did not know that each step of Jack was heavier with the dimensions of his own aiguille, the child's convulsions and amusement wedded in his ears but evaporated against the growing darkness of his cadaverous thoughts.

His perished head saw the world differently, disconnected from the beauty of his son's impeccability, consumed by a mental state that distorts reality and isolated him from everything he once cared about, it was over for him. He would jump into a moving train, with a fierce conflicted ebb in his eyes, the world around him cold and devoid of compassion, no immediate adjacent stranger to talk him out of it, as the jarring sound of the train approached, leaving both him and the untroubled son paralyzed. The only thing he had planned to leave behind was a broken family, and a short letter of justification and acknowledgment on social media.

The effectiveness of British Transport Police at the scene of any accident is less spoken off; however, this should be well-regarded, and mimicked by other nations especially Africa. Their remarkable characterizations by their structured approach, dedicated professionalism, and emphasis on public safety is wildly admired. The weeks that would follow blotch a long walk from home: filled with recuperation for both the father and son, clutched pain and overwhelming despair, as well as months of lengthy days of court cases and in-and-out bandits from confinement center and incarceration for the father as he had attempted a murder of his child.

The church that famously lectured about the importance of the return of the prodigal son turned their back on one of their own. They in one way or another, either they were aware or too late to grasp, in small or big faction, assisted in changing decades long instrumentalist to a one-day individual involved in a failed murder-suicide attempt. The appalling incongruity part was that, these same faces of adherents of the Gospel that renounced and disowned him, at a point of reparation, would rush to the Queen Elizabeth Hospital, Glasgow, upon hearing the unpleasant breaking news to grieve with his family. That doesn't seem quite accurate.

I would not hesitate to label them as insincere if they truly were, but I am confident that such a description does not apply to them. Most of them have driven me around in their private cars even when I did not ask especially in my early days after service. Some of them cooked me local foods before my tongue adapted to the foreign cuisines of Korean Bibimpap, German Bavaria Brauhaus and Maki and Ramen to a site where I could gather cooking resources and engineer my signature chicken centered foods.

Deep down they are good people probably blood hounded and leveraged with a sort of worldly begrudged indoctrination. I know they had not switched off their sense of belongingness when Jack needed them. Perhaps, they had been restricted by certain unidentifiable and unscriptural modern blockages—an unspoken, collective mindset akin to a "let's crucify him" convocation, reminiscent of the teachings that led to the stoning of the apostles in the Bible.

The exact reasons remain uncertain, what I do know is that; Their inherent goodness would surface in the aftermath, as they gathered at his home—not only to donate generous provisions, inspirational gift cards and heaps worth of foods for him and his family but would formulate a prayer cathedral around the debacle. That is community. That is compassion. That is the church.

But why wait for the fallout? Why not support the individual from the outset and avert the collapse entirely? Why not embrace the person right away and prevent things from falling apart? That is the place civilization is in the current state of the Rabbi's house. This is not a place of live and abundance, it only exists in theorical words.

We have become saints with a frown. We have close joyful hearts and that have closed the curtains of hope. The teachings of the Holy Spirit have become showmanship. The endangered people have been exposed and stoned. As precious as the soul of every person is either a believer or not, in today's temple, the diminutive moment you fall back, the unscrupulous people go against you, provide fabricated reasons for your lynching and your premature termination heedless that the aliveness of people provides a fascinating commentary on the Gospel.

Those in charge in many of these churches are absentminded to the core that, they have tempered with the rules of the game of righteousness.

Most of them have disregarded the everlasting golden rule of *love thy neighbor like yourself* and forgotten that attackable and vulnerable members are huge illustrations of the Good News that Jesus brought to humanity: God, the father who cares, and loves everyone with boundless passion and idolization.

From the home country of the First Lady of the United States Melania Trump, Slovenia to the coffee-growing landscapes of Gustavo Petro's Columbia bubbled up to the boisterous diverse ecosystems of Anthony Albanese's Australia, the church appears to be engaging in political advocacy and cancel culture that sometimes aligns with certain political powers and hoax agendas. This institution for all mankind now plays identity politics.

The Zanzibaris do not mingle or associate with the Zaragozans. And there are sixteen sub groups within the internal wings especially among the strings of vocalists, there is no unity only disunity. Thesis long chastisements and assessments on gender roles and treatment of women have been skyrocketed. Most of these women are not only incredibly competent and nobler than their male counterparts but carry the anointing and grace of Kathryn Kuhlman particularly in the faculty of ordination and leadership.

Meanwhile they have been forced to bury their talents because the modern-day churches do not fathom for women to be spiritual leaders of the faith and have been mellowed to caretakers and reduced to the backseat. Indigenous spiritual practices are suppressed, and the spread of European non- Christianized ways have taken over at the expense of heavenly local cultures and scriptural governance. Those who speak in the languages of the spirit are deemed to be rhetorically mad.   I am inclined to state that after the rock-hewn tomb that was sealed by a large stone, and was guarded by Roman soldiers to preclude any tampering by external interference or curious walkers from going in, was opened, and Christ resurrected from the death; the people might have thought that he lost his innovative prowess for modern Christianity not in his shroud but the nail holes in his right and left hands. Jumped number of church leaders have been accused of amassing wealth, living in opulent residences, squandering on extravagant projects, notwithstanding the classic holidays in Las Vagas, the playground of America rather than using the temple funds on charitable and equitable works. People no longer have Bibles in their homes.

Gender mutilations are been undertaken by couple regular surgeons in the church. Big pharma and Big Christian Hospital networks have covered up horrific long term side effects of sex transitions in order to get rich at the expense of those without protection and weapons. Tampons are mandatory in the male section restroom of many churches across the United Kingdom and Europe. Everybody gossips within the organization. There are no signs of stretching strategies for members to thrive and meet the targets of this generation and the subsequent generations to come in this ever — changing human advancement.

I can vividly picture the profound yet haunting words of John 11:35 unfolding once more. This time, however, the contrast is stark—the Son of Man may not come with mercy. Though His heart is eternally filled with forgiveness, peace, and prosperity—not just the sorrow of parables for those who reject Him—there's a palpable shift. I sense a reckoning, fierce and unrelenting, akin to Daenerys Targaryen astride Drogon, unleashing a torrent of flames that razed a city to ashes, scattering its people, creations, and creatures into oblivion. A scene of total annihilation.

CHAPTER FIVE:

IMMIGRATION IS THE ENVY OF THE WORLD

"Now the Lord said to Abram,
Go from your country and your kindred and
Your father's house to the land that I will show you.
And I will make of you a great nation, and
I will bless you, and make your name great,
so that you will be a blessing.
I will bless those who bless you,
and him who curses you
I will curse; and by you all the families of
the earth shall bless themselves. "
Genesis 12: 1-3

I was prompted to not posit because it was hundred percent guaranteed to be unthinkable. Even the best ones could not do it. I was doubted to open the channels. These attacks were normal. People are always a hindrance to themselves. Life is tough, get a helmet. I had tumbled from the first floor to the ground, barely surviving the fall. I had crossed many seas. I was a first generation. Before that, I was among the top one percent not just in my high school science class, or my batch but overall, since the inception of the thought of the local leaders to build that secondary school. You can ask around! In fact, we are the premium. My batch made unprecedented history. The pacesetters!

Nobler men, remunerative investors and government agencies did not only flood-in their big wallets but indisputably opted to educate their kids there and appealed to their neighbors both next-door and abroad to do so; in a community where people convened for pipe borne running water all day and night long. The water coloration ranging from powdered white at dawn to cylindrical spirogyra jumping in it at dusk. Caprice!

I did it in a course I sought and fought

for under extraordinary constraints. I began the school itself in the subservient academic semester of first year, and not the traditional first semester. I missed matriculation and meet the press orientations. This delay was borne of financial constraints and the grief that gripped my family after the untimely passing of my brother Kingsley that November. Bereaved and burdened, my parents insisted I attend a local school within the community, rejecting my aspiration to study in a more prestigious institution in the city. It was a compromise I initially refused, opting instead to remain at home.

After much persuasion from my mother, I acquiesced. Even then, the path was far from straightforward. I would be denied a seat in the coveted science stream due to oversubscription; I found myself placed in agricultural studies. Undeterred, I worked tirelessly to identify opportunities for transition, ultimately securing my place in the science program midway through the semester—a feat that felt nothing short of miraculous.

I remained restless and uncertain until one pivotal day when our chemistry teacher, Mr. Ushao addressed the class. With calm yet profound conviction, he said, *"School isn't defined by its buildings or location; it's about you—the individual—and your willingness to learn."* Those words resonated deeply, cutting through my doubts and sparking a newfound resolve. Perhaps it was a routine speech he delivered to every incoming class, a casual remark made in passing, or even a subtle endorsement of the school to bolster his own pride.

Whatever his intention, to me, it was nothing short of a game-changing moment that completely redefined my perspective. Mr. Apraku Johnson, the Assistant Head Master of Academic ludicrously said "your boy is unstoppably crazy," I responded, amid my dad in his office, "either that or I follow my dad to his farm". They both laughed uncontrollably. They became friends and carried on their unhoped-for consonance till Today. Huge respect to the space of agriculturalists. That was a bold statement from a village boy with a city dream, who just wanted something bad, and not to defame the importance of agronomy in our world.

These attacks were emitted from all the four cardinal points, in and around the space of the nuclear family, friends and fireworks. I proceeded anywhere. I was victorious and like every other groovy scenario: they shamelessly did a meteoric one-eighty, with stunned remarks and sham commentaries: that's my man! this is how we do it! this is what I talked about!

Confidentially, I would go, you sure dude? Followed by, an honest sigh! The persona of the year 2022 was a composition of obstacles and global glitches. Global economies faced inflation due to a combination of pandemic recovery, supply chain disruptions, and the war in Ukraine. Energy and food prices soared, affecting many nations. Citizens took to the streets of Accra to demand better economic policies and accountability from the government. Protests organized by groups like *Arise Ghana* highlighted concerns over its government introduction of a new tax policy called the Electronic Transfer Levy (E-Levy) which imposed a 1.5% tax on digital financial transactions, including Mobile Money (MoMo) payments.

The tax intended to raise revenue and help reduce Ghana's debt faced strong opposition from citizens, who viewed it as regressive and harmful to small businesses and lower-income households that rely on the industrial logic of MoMo transactions across Africa. Queen Elizabeth II passed away after a 70-year reign, leading to King Charles III's ascension. British Prime Minister Boris Johnson resigned amid scandals, and Liz Truss briefly served before Rishi Sunak took over and will go on to lose landslide to the Keir Stammer Labour Party. It had been three decades since the academics took over the federal reserve in many developed countries.

The Supreme Court of the United States' reversal of Roe v. Wade sparked institutional debates in Oxford Union etc. Elon Musk acquired Twitter, baptized and renamed it X, gave free speech its voice, leading to changes in the platform and major staff layoffs and completely handed over the media privileges to the individuals which would play inadvertently a spiritual role in the reelection in President Trump in November 2024.

It was a Wednesday morning, and the long-awaited email slayed in with a swaggered attention, for a second, the world narrowed down to that sound, and I felt a rush of anticipation, with an alert that the decision desk of UKIV has arrived at a decision and my passport were ready for collection. I gave a super nod: not the characteristic one that the average person on the street, sees a fellow and jerks the head downward first like the movement of the diaphragm during inhalation, but the other one where the head is tilted to the occipital direction and stands still facing north. There was order and chaos in the ballroom.

The pretzel on schedule was even though, I couldn't warrant an outcome, I was confident like Julius Caesar as he mobilized the courage and crossed the Rubicon and entered Rome with his forbidden army. Caesar's actions might have embodied his intense self-assurance, nourished by years of military victories, political alliances, and a deep understanding of Rome's politics; mine was sponsored by a great measure of grace, and raw optimism.

For most people from low-income countries, that small sticker in the center of a passport page holds the weight of dreams, struggles, and endless aspirations. It felt almost unreal, as this simple piece of documentation could bridge the gap between a lifetime of imagining and the beginning of an unknown adventure. I was deeply humbled.

As I set out on my journey to the West, I was faced with electrifying options, each offering its own promise. Among them were three strong contenders: the bold, ambitious American Dream of 2022, filled with endless possibilities; the calm, progressive nature of the Netherlands, offering balance and innovation; and the United Kingdom, rich in history and intellectual pursuit, with its mix of tradition and modern opportunity. Each path seemed to hold a different future, magnetic pull and the decision ahead felt as daunting as it was exciting. In the end, what mattered most was which place could be the launchpad for my next big adventure. I chose Great Britain. The stunning landscapes and vibrant colors of the flag of Scotland which somehow had my favorite blue and white childhood colors and the free entry across major famous cities of the world like Manchester and London added an extra layer of excitement. I imagined how it would be like to walk on the grasses of the Queen's Buckingham Palace and the pavements of Westminster Abbey, which I did and was finally able to cross them from me many to do checklists.

Unlike most people, I do not only have a roster, I have a lifelong index, and every passing minute or months brings its own steadiness to it. It's a catalog that transcends from the individual weaned around my family and friends and do not end on the national level but the footstool of Gods mandate.

The United Kingdom felt like the perfect fit, and, in turn, it welcomed me as if it had been calling my name-Victor Carson all along. I thought about my brother, Kingsley, the third child of my parents, who had been taken from us at the age of twenty-three in the summer of 2012, just three days after he had received his travel documents to the United States. It hit me hard, the cruel irony of it all. He had waited so long for that opportunity, spent years dreaming of a life abroad, only to have it snatched away in an instant.

I thought about how much effort my father had poured into securing those travel papers, navigating through a maze of bureaucracy and uncertainty, just to see his son's dream come to fruition- only for it and the son himself to slip through our fingers at the unpardonable mistake of a berserk doctor. I couldn't help but reflect on what my journey would mean back home. The young boys in the village would notice my absence, their curiosity would grow, and soon enough, they would begin to drill my parents about my whereabouts.

What would they think when they heard that I had gone to a place they could only imagine? I thought about how much power my decision carried, not just for me, but for my family, for the village desperado boys, and for the generations who would follow.

I thought about the land of Churchill, Great Britain, a place I had only ever seen through the lens of a television screen or within the pages of the books I had devoured, painting my own version of that distant world in my mind. And now, it was no longer a far-off dream; it was within my reach. The freedom, the opportunities, the chance to be part of a history much bigger than myself, it was all there, waiting for me. In that moment, my systema nervosum, was overwhelmed and flushed with something deeply profound about the chance to walk in spaces where great minds had once stood, to step into a world that had shaped so much of the history I had studied, and yet here I was, a part of that story.

I carried with me the burden of my brother's unfulfilled dream, the sacrifices of my parents, and the hope of what my journey could mean not just for me, but for the young boys back in the village. This wasn't just my opportunity, it was ours. And with that, I felt a deep sense of gratitude and responsibility, humbled by the path that lay ahead.

As I walked out of the Movenpick Hotel, the warm afternoon air hit me, before making my way through the noisy surroundings, I stood at the lobby and phoned my dad about the news. His voice at the other tale: every word seems to lift, filled with newfound energy and possibility. It was brighter, more animated, with a bit of wonder- as if he was still absorbing the good fortune, savoring each word, letting it settle in.

The hotel's grand exterior quickly petered out behind me as I moved towards the roadside, where the busy purr and warble of the city took over.

The street was alive with the sound of honking cars, chatter, and the rhythm of a typical daily life in an-always-busy Accra, everyone hoping to get something into their bellies by the close of the day. I navigated the sidewalk, my steps purposeful, knowing that a cab was just ahead to gather me home.

Unlike Changi International Airport of Singapore that continued its robust COVID-19 restrictions until October 2022 before taking that significant tramp to fully reopen its economy with trouble-free and straightforward entry requirements for travelers, the Kotoka International Airport of Ghana was long functioning. Named after Lieutenant General Emmanuel Kotoka, a Ghanaian military officer, the airport has grown into a hub of West African travel with its sleek architectural designs and improved amenities influenced by global standards and subtle Ghanaian heritage.

The airport itself displays a blend of adventure and organized chaos; people rushing, announcements not only running over the speakers in English Language without any translation to the local Ghanaian language to whom it may concern but pulling air passengers, both first timers and regulars over like an American white supremacist policeman who probably got divorced by his wife the night before and had seen a black man in a demon car, the scent of duty-free perfume and coffee midair.

Boarding time approached and it inserted an emotional state into my accompanying family. Godspeed Victor! There was a quick blink from my left eye to them, silent but loaded with love. Security was swift, professional and intense. I taxied my way to my ceremonial seat after tucking away my backpack. Caprice! Fastened my seat belt under instructions by an air hostess in a uniform perfectly pressed, her movement smooth and fluid, a depiction of the years of experience and poise she had cultivated as she walked the aisle.

The engine roared to life on the tarmac as the plane lifted up like a domestic dove, as if gravity itself was letting go of me in the aftermath of the piloting pep talk. I was reminded of Newton's Laws of motion that, I had studied in physics class at high school, along with those thoughts were the deep generation of nudge and faith in this marvel of engineering; a complex system of metal, technology, turbines, force of air currents powered by human ingenuity as a liminal environment suspended between two worlds, both physical and existential.

I was struck by the reminiscences of two horrendous events first: the incident of April 10, 2010, when Polish President Lech Kaczyński and his wife died in a bang when they were attempting to land at Smolensk North Airport in Russia, and second, in 2018, Lion Air Flight 610, a Boeing 737 Max 8, crashed into the Java Sea just minutes after takeoff from Jakarta, claiming the lives of all 189 passengers and crew on board. I shook it off.

I opted to fly with Emirates Airways, partly because of my admiration for Real Madrid and Vini Jr, the best player in the world. There was something noteworthy about being on the same airline that shares its legacy with such a legendary football club. It felt like a small connection, a nod to my loyalty to the team, as if the same level of excellence and prestige that Real Madrid embodies extended to the airline as well. I was also amused by a contemplation that popped in my head, that considering it's being a Muslim-run airline, the probabilities of an Arab passenger talking a fellow countryman out of any catastrophic ideas might be higher.

I bowed my head, said a prayer, and hoisted it back up, like an African Jedi, ready to conquer Great Britain. Caprice!
I would do a three-hour layover in the vast, extravagant Dubai airport, a place almost like a city in itself. As I step off the plane, I'll scan the signs, orienting myself in this labyrinth of gleaming shops and towering glass. With each turn, I would be drawn in by the airport's grandeur, yet focused on the goal-navigating my way to the gate for my connecting flight to Glasgow. The moment the plane began its descent into Glasgow, my heart quickened. Below me, the vast green expanse of the British land stretched out, with rolling hills and scattered towns emerging through the clouds. It was surreal, this landscape I had only seen in pictures and stories, now unfolding beneath me in real-time.

The buildings and roads were smaller than I imagined, but the sense of history, of something ancient and enduring, was unmistakable. It felt like the edge of a new world, the beginning of something I had only dreamed of. As the wheels touched the macadam, there was a brief moment of stillness, followed by the rush of the plane coming to a halt. I could almost actualize the muscle of the journey, the distance traveled in sixteen hours and the teeth of what lay ahead.

The doors opened, and I walked off the plane, taking my first steps on British soil.

The Scottish breeze was a sharp contrast to the warmth I had left behind, and I inhaled deeply as I made my way out to another dimension of immigration standpoint. The queue seemed endless on the route for any other passport holders from the rest of the world contrary to that reserved for foreigners from Canada, America, Australia and Brites themselves; but with each step toward the desk, the reality of this new chapter became more tangible. The immigration officer's questions were simple, but they carried a quiet importance. After a brief exchange, my passport was stamped, and in that instant, I was officially a legal resident of the Great Britain.

I was cladded in a navy-blue suit, my stomach empty and aching from hours of travel as my adaptive features for the food served on board were prematurely off.

I made my way to the baggage claim, the floor highly ordered and well brushed by workers in blue vests. No frantic rush, no cluttered voices, no chaos just the steady intone of the luggage retrieval area. Bags were glided along the conveyor belt; I waited for mine. I stepped out of the terminal and onto the unfamiliar streets of Glasgow, instantly feeling like I was starring in my own version of "Lost in Translation." There was no crowd waiting to embrace me, no familiar faces or comforting voices to welcome me. Just me, my small suitcase and 200 liquids in my wallet and for the first time, I truly discerned the solitude but soldiered it off.

My cellphone had powered down. I climbed into a black cab, and the usual sidemirror excursion took over. The city unmasked; the sleet on high-rises, the steadily elevated road signs, McDonald's drive thru, the silent honks of vehicles, the industrial sense kicked in, pedestrians swarming along, wrapped in coats against the cool, mostly humid air, and their accents floating around, thick and warm, adding to the city's character etc. Unparalleled, I felt like I was living in a movie where the subtitles didn't quite match the scene. I arrived at my formerly arranged residence by the great memorization of my postcode. I had little understanding of the relevance of the postcode system in the West and how it functioned.

Where I was coming from, destinations were marked mainly by paintings of buildings and towers of heaps beside electricity transformers. I would later learn more about it and other essential amenities like securing my UK bank accounts, purchasing minutes on Next bike and capturing my address in my curriculum vitae in my first week. After I entered my new execute suite, I unlocked my necktie and my waistbelt, dropped my belongings on the bed and lifted up my hands above my hairline like a Jude

Bellingham celebration and proudly sung aloud the popular song of John Denver, "Country Roads, Take Me Home." Caprice!

I recall one of those early days when I ventured out to Tesco for my weekly groceries. On my way back, disaster slapped—my carrier bag ripped apart, sending oranges and onions tumbling onto the rain-slicked road. They scattered in every direction, rolling away as if mocking my predicament. To make matters worse, the rain gassed up, and the traffic lights were about to turn red, signaling the cars to surge forward. For a moment I froze. It wasn't the risk of bending down in the middle of the road that held me back; it was the thought of what might follow.

The potential headline for BBC Scotland loomed vividly in my mind: "Immigrant from Africa hit by car while chasing onions and oranges in the street." What haunted me even more wasn't how my family back home would receive the tragic news, but the reactions and affronts, comments and judgements, I imagined facing from strangers and onlookers here.

That day, I made an executive decision: I walked away, leaving the scattered groceries behind. I may not have eaten that night, but as I lay in bed, I found solace in knowing I could always replace the groceries the next day. More importantly, I got to sleep in my own bed, free of any dramatic consequences, unwanted bandages or regret over a moment gone awry.

❖❖❖

The ruling class across the United Kingdom from His majesty Naval Base Clyde of Scotland, to the neo-Gothic Houses of Parliament tower over the River Thames of England, to the solidified dynasty of Wales; share several key characteristics, despite differing regional identities and ideological perspicacity.

I grew up reading the stories of Margaret Thatcher and the people of her time with their true conservatism, free markets economy with limited government intervention and zero tolerance to perniciousness.

Much like the contemporary political figures— Boris Johnson, Liz Truss, and Keir Starmer, Iron Lady's background was rooted in an education that went beyond the academic, into the realm of power itself. Eton, Harrow, and other elite institutions weren't just places of learning; they were the crucibles where future rulers were forged, where the delicate balance of tradition, duty, and privilege was ingrained into every word spoken and every decision made.

The breeding grounds for subtle art of making the best connections over brandy-soaked debates in private clubs. The values instilled were often less about the pursuit of wisdom and more about knowing how to navigate the corridors of power with a perfectly steamed suit, a well-timed joke, and a well-placed nod to history.

Whilst African leaderships in the era of 1980s was thrusted into leadership facilities with little formal training, frequently and habitually learning on the job technicalities, evolving in response to challenges, characterized by trial and error, shaped largely by external pressures and the immediacy of crisis, those in the British elite were meticulously cultivated from a young age. Their education was not just erudite and collegiate; it was a deliberate process of socialization into power. From their infantry years, they were trained to speak eloquently, debate effectively, and think critically about reform and governance. By the time they reached adulthood, they were already seasoned in the art of leadership, having been prepared for it all their lives.

I wandered through the streets of Glasgow, Grimsby and Gateshead and the variations and imbalances emerged and became painfully undeniable, between the men and women of these two different continents - Africa and Europe and their massive pragmatic contributions to their nations. I became aware of my surrounding with each rising star and a prepping morning including the remarkable duality of the Scottish people and their sense of intelligent humor, witnessed and appreciated in my mentor and friend Sir Iain MacInnes.

Like most Scottish people, Sir Iain carries centuries of tradition like a torch, illuminating both a fierce independence and an openness that welcomes a stranger to their world. Those I have met from Bearsden to Baillieston or from King's Park to Kirkintilloch; are rooted in history but agile in spirit and bound by an unspoken philosophy of resilience and community, weathering life's storms with an unwavering determination and a sense of knowing when to pause and have some good fun.

There is a quiet strength in their pride, a respect for the land that has shaped them, and an instinct for generosity that often hides behind a dry wit and candid demeanor. The Scottish people either a native young girl gallivanting around Buchanan Galleries or a veteran on CityLink bus from Edinburgh to Clydebank: each carries a unique authenticity, valuing life not for its comforts but for the hardiness required to face both winter's chill and life's greater trials.

They are, at heart, a fascinating paradox, grounded still adventurous, traditional but forward-looking. Their outlook on life reflects a blend of uncommon wisdom and modern insight, each day lived with a sense of loyalty, friendship, and a profound depth that gives others a helping hand while remaining unmistakably and unapologetically their own.

Over the weeks, I would find myself acclimating to the Western way of life - the unspoken codes, the subtleties woven into daily interactions, the textures of a culture that feels both familiar and rarely foreign. New friendships and weekend plans would emerge, bridging generations and necessary commitments; each one offering a skirmish frame into the unfiltered realities of those who have navigated this landscape for far longer durations than me and the youthful ones who only think about amusement parks and the latest Louis Vuitton.

Through their injunctions, I would begin to perceive the sharp polarity between the romanticized narratives I had once read and the complex, mostly contradictory truths on the streets of Glasgow. The flips of the historical books offered tales of triumph, progress, and steadfast leadership chronicles of a nation that had meticulously crafted its legacy through discipline, intellect, and vision.

Amidst the everyday croon of the city, that legacy obscurely felt intangible, as if those stories belonged to a parallel world. The streets breathed with a different rhythm, one that spoke of toughness in lieu privilege, adaptation instead of control. There was a rawness here, an authenticity not reflected in the carefully curated accounts of history. The monuments and architecture hinted at past glories, but the daily struggles of those who walked beneath them recounted a yam of grit, of endurance-values less often celebrated in pages but woven deeply into the fabric of the present.

The ideals preserved in books signaled remote, almost abstract, disconnected from the ordinary lives unfolding before me. There were no guarantees. There were no certainties. The elites may have adorned the luxury of mapping out their futures and dandled over the transcripts and reproductive documentations of todays and the times ahead in the lockers of their brick walled vacated offices and classified Panama papers.

However, the people I encounter on the bustling side streets of Glasgow city center near the JP Morgan Chase building, those I see through the tinted windows of their lavish yet heavily financed vehicles in Newcastle, or the patrons gathered outside a noisy pub in Manchester, drowning their dreams one drink at a time, tell a different story. So, too, do those on the other end of the line, seeking support through benefit claims in Middlesbrough, or the confused immigrant in Stratford, London, struggling to navigate the tube system. They suggest lives governed by reactionary mandates and constant adjustments—people merely getting by. Among them, a shrinking number are deemed survivalists, even within the credentialed workforce—the backbone of any great nation.

This muddles within me a profound and protracted sense of solemn reflection, one that is heavy with melancholy and tinged with disappointment. It is a pressure that presses on the soul, a disdain ache that stretches through time, as I search for answers in a world that once seemed so full of rewards and competence.

What has truly become of the great United Kingdom, once a beacon of boundless promise and power? What became of Winston Churchill's vision—a dream that once seemed so certain, so inevitable? This was the nation that, after God's creation of the world, carried a divine torch—a guiding light not only for itself but for all humanity, leading the way toward progress and advancement. Britain once stood as the architect of modern civilization, its legacy of enlightenment, exploration, and innovation illuminating the path for nations across the globe.

As I write this book, ensnared in the intricate and molecular galaxies of contemplation, I cannot disregard the pervasive sense of loss that subtly infiltrates every thought. Where has the once-unyielding determination, the strategic clarity that followed the televised coverage of

Her Majesty the Queen Elizabeth's coronation on June 2, 1953, broadcasting a moment of profound significance to millions across the globe. The royal procession, adorned with grand ceremonial regalia, smudging the dawn of a new era.

Black-and-white scenes flickered across screens, families mustering around their televisions, and being drawn into the gravitas of the occasion and noticing the motivating force of that young home-schooled woman who had the world resting on her shoulders like Merlin, though, his was envisioned in a land of magic and myth.

In that transitory moment, bestowed with the glories and golden emblem, smoothened by the collective optimism of a nation, her nation poised on the cusp of transformation, maintained fueled progression, navigated adversity, and constructed the global bedded order. The United Kingdom of the late 1900s now exists as a subdued fragile echo, scarcely detectable against the backdrop of today's global landscape. It's as if the country decided to take a nap, only to wake up and wonder where all the excitement went, finding itself staring at a reality that feels a bit too surreal to grasp.

The once dynamic spirit of stolid ambition which defined its course, has been redressed by an insubstantial reverberation, a ghostly bombination of formal prestige mimicking the sibilate of an electric fan that has long surrendered its battle against the heat in a small corner storeroom reserved for harvested maize in the Mahalapye village of Botswana.

Major Cooperation like the Britain Broadcasting Cooperation is deteriorating at a rapid rate if not stalled. The BBC's subscription model, which is uniquely enforced through the UK's mandatory TV license, has become a point of contention among many Britons and UK residents.

Something that used to be regarded as a foundational pillar of British culture-offering reliable news, quality dramas, and educational programming, the legacy media role and funding model have been fundamentally re-evaluated through the lens of a rapidly evolving media landscape.

In a shifting age of digital dynamics where streaming options abound, the BBC's mandatory fee strikes many as an obligation rather than a voluntary choice. Younger audiences who prioritize personalized, on-demand features are now exposed to character compromising television shows on their polarized multiple channels and everyone is apathetic to it.

The new brand of censorship, in its quiet omnipresence, has become a misanthropic tool that channels conversations into authoritarian regimen vagueness of acceptable forms, making true intellectual freedom a pursuit, rather than a right for the civilians. There is a high stake of an individual to hear a certain knock at his door due to an arbitrary post made on online networking, in the land that prides itself on freedom and free speech. Salmonella and campylobacter are for sale simultaneously in the supermarkets like Tesco, Lidl, Sainsbury's and other bodega corner stores across the nation meanwhile Food Standards Authority (FSA) and other regulatory bodies are tolerating lapses and indirectly succoring the unappeasable campaign metrics of food borne diseases and condemning it on budget constraints and filibusters. Consumption protection is broken in especially large supply chains of foods like chicken and dairy where volume and cost pressures have sabotaged the quality.

Nigel Farage is not as divisive as propagandists might have you believe. He represents a unique blend of state loyalty and a willingness to challenge the status quo, advocating not only for British interests but also for national sovereignty and free-market policies across neighboring regions. However, attributing the UK's contemporaneous challenges—such as economic turbulence, logistical issues at ports like Dover and Milford Haven, the Grenfell Tower fire that tragically claimed nearly a hundred lives and exposed critical flaws in social housing and fire safety standards, or the swift resignation of Archbishop Justin Welby of Canterbury, who crowned King Charles III, amid allegations of covering up an infamous abuse scandal—entirely to Farage's strong advocacy for Brexit and his outspoken rhetoric would be an oversimplification.

Solar power poised to be the vast majority of power remains sidelined among the distresses. Meanwhile, energy companies continue to disrupt power supplies during the harsh winter months, disproportionately affecting vulnerable populations unable to afford inflated energy bills. This ongoing neglect underscores a profound systemic failure to balance long-term sustainability with the pressing humanitarian needs of today.

The HM Treasury stands in silence, as the financial giants promise a breathing space to their clients, offering hope on one hand, yet tightening the noose of credit scores with the other. In this quiet theatre of broken promises, the script is written by those who wield power, and the actors-the unsuspecting customers - are left to play their parts in a drama of empty assurances.

The National Health Service is been privatized closing the doors to those without wealth and posing more risks to accessibility and affordability, and making way for profitability. If you reside in the UK, hope you don't get sick, your GP local long queues will make you deep think over your daily choices.

The National Citizen Service, once a cornerstone

for fostering unity among youth across varied backgrounds, ethnicities, faiths, and identities, has now been abruptly dismantled under the Labour Party's direction led by Sir Keir Starmer. This decision disbands an organization that nurtured cross-cultural understanding, leaving a void in efforts to bridge societal divides for the next generation.

Working-class individuals, particularly the younger generation, are encountering formidable obstacles in accessing the property market, often compelled to resort to transient or precarious rental options that lack both security and the promise of permanence.

Racist chants ring through UK sports stadiums with troubling regularity; however, perpetrators frequently escape accountability, casting a shadow over the efforts to promote inclusivity and respect in sports. Innocent people continue to fall victim to street stabbings across the major cities of Liverpool and Blackpool with tangible ownership often absence leading to a legion of unsettling trends. Productivity across many local forums and urban organizations has taken a significant hit due to the rise of remote work.

In a country, where the lines between personal and professional lives are increasingly blurred, even the most influential positions are not immune in the state. Unlike the Iron Lady who worked through her lunch, the Prime Minister, once a figure synonymous with eventful office works and strategic meetings, now works from the comfort of home, embodying the shift in professional dynamics.

The lecturer, once accustomed to lecturing in front of eager students, now holds classes from the comfort of his bed, in his unwashed pants and sweaty shirts blurring the sanctity of work and rest. Soon the delivery driver and the surgeon would be tempted to follow suit if nothing substantial is taken into account.

Farmers are treated as peasants; work physically demanding, long hours requirements and enduring unpredictable weather pattern, yet their efforts are often undervalued by both the public and government. Wages remain stagnant, but bus fares in the UK have just been increased an absurd disparity that further burdens everyday commuters.

While countries like the United States of America charge ahead with ambition and innovation, prioritizing entrepreneurial spirit and future-focused initiatives, like Starlink, the world's most advanced satellite technology delivering highest ever seen form of internet etc., the UK often seems bogged down by a heavy focus on regulation and preservation of the past. Here, the emphasis on safeguarding tradition and maintaining complex regulatory frameworks has created an environment where new ideas can feel stifled before they even begin.

The abundance of regulatory bodies

imposes layers of oversight that can drain energy and resources, lowering the stakes of entrepreneurship and dulling the momentum of new ventures. Instead of inspiring bold risks and innovation, this approach often leads to businesses that proceed cautiously, navigating hoops rather than pushing boundaries. By placing a high premium on watchfulness and historical continuity, the UK risks missing out on the dynamism and economic growth that come from fostering a more liberated, forward-focused entrepreneurial environment.

I have visited a few historical cultural centers in the great UK, from the famous British Museum in London to the unfamous McManus: Dudee's Art Gallery and Museum; walking through any British heritage exhibition can feel like being led through a stale, highly curated narrative that clings desperately to relics of Britain's military history.

The spaces are packed with artifacts from old conflicts, walls lined with arms and armor that idealize eras of empire, world wars, and colonial dominance. Rather than upstanding and embracing a forward-looking view, British institutions seem intent on grounding visitors in a dated vision of the past, encouraging a nostalgia for Britain's global influence instead of fostering insight into its complexities. These exhibits often seem less like a bridge to understanding and more like a stage set for historical glorification, a constant reminder of past power and conquest rather than a balanced provocation.

The experience can be suffused with an overemphasis on valor and sacrifice, while sidestepping the darker sides of empire. The displays suggest an almost uncritical reverence, focusing on grandeur and legacy but leaving little room for a more nuanced consideration of the impacts and consequences of these histories. Instead of engaging visitors with a balanced view of the country's evolution, British museums often offer a single-minded celebration of "heritage" that risks obscuring other essential truths.

Reform Party Minister Rupert Lowe publicly hooted on X that, "we need a British Elon Musk", the sad reality is that there are countless of them, just that we aren't allowed to pursue ambition. The rural areas of the great UK are crime scheme hotspots today, and a case study tomorrow in Oxford Union debates. The modern UK workplace has taken on an almost absurdist quality, where the boundaries between professionalism and personal indulgence have blurred into something unrecognizable.

Picture this: an office, once a sanctuary of discipline and intellect, now punctuated by the jarring barks and bounding leaps of dogs and cats. This is no longer merely a workspace but a curious cross between an animal husbandry experiment and a leisure lounge. This happened to me: few days back, I got startled by the huge bark of a bull dog in the office, and the owner went, sorry, and laughed off, I just looked at her with a Dwayne Johnson smoldering intensity look.

What was once a pursuit of excellence has, in many quarters, devolved into a pursuit of comfort, regardless of its impact on productivity. There is also this philosophical conundrum: the tension between ideals of inclusivity and the erosion of rigor. Leftist notions, with their roots in empathy and equity, have sprouted policies that, while well-meaning, have inadvertently traded competence for consensus and vigor for complacency.

The result is a workplace culture increasingly allergic to accountability, where intellectual robustness is almost sacrificed at the altar of trends and sensitivities. I am a fulltime black man. My grandfather was black, my future kids will still be black, I don't care about it, what matters is competence and character, the broader implications of this drift are staggering, as it wanes, so too does the economic vitality of the nation.

Trams are experiencing a global renaissance, with the exception of Britain, they are dismissed as prohibitively expensive because most funds are already packaged in proxy wars.   This perception, entrenched in council chambers and within Whitehall, whistles an ovate and a broader challenge: a national tendency to over-engineer infrastructure and treat each project as a bespoke endeavor. Such an approach drives up costs unnecessarily, making otherwise viable projects appear unattainable, but totally unfair to the greatest civilization in the world human history.

The promises of a better life in Great Britain and the West now reveal a troubling contradiction. Many individuals from Africa, Asia, and the Middle East who departed their homelands, not driven by ambition alone, but by a commitment to make it to the top, support and uplift the communities they left behind, now find themselves forsaken in foreign lands, reduced to begging or eking out an existence as outcasts on the streets and in the stations of cities like London and Londonderry. The greener pastures have swallowed them, regurgitated, only to consume them again. Those who have decided not to give up are only hanging in there.

This is not the UK I was promised, where opportunities were the hallmarks as enormous as the rain that falls on our green hills. I was told a land of prosperity, where dreams could run wilder and freer like a good old-fashioned British road trip. But now, it feels more like the nation's out of petrol, stuck at a dead-end roundabout, trying to figure out which direction to go next. President Ronald Reagan might have quipped, "I didn't sign up for this! I thought I was getting a Rolls-Royce, not a rusted-out bike tortoise!" and definitely not a nation succumbed to its own eccentricities.

CHAPTER SIX:

GOOD HEALTH IS A DISTANT MEMORY

*"Beloved,
I pray that all may go well with you
and that you may be in good health,
as it goes well with your soul."*
3 John 1 : 2

I t was a quiet evening in our home in Ghana, the kind of evening that felt both unfamiliar and routine. My mother, the second-in-command of our household, was busy preparing dinner at the front of the house, cooking on a tripod stove over an open flame. We didn't have a proper kitchen—just an outdoor space where she made sure we had enough food for the days to come.

The rich aroma of her soup and stew filled the ambience and dictated the rhythmicity of the day like North Korea regulating the freedom of thoughts and expression of its people. Comforting me as I sat nearby, reflecting on the recent completion of my university studies.

I was waiting for my placement to begin as a Teaching Assistant at the medical school, a portfolio that I was both eager and anxious to step into. In a moment that felt as if it came from a nightmare, everything changed. While Mom was tending to the pot, stirring the soup with the same meticulousness she always did, she suddenly called out to me, her voice sharp and urgent. "Hold my hand!" she yelled. I rushed to her side, along with my brother Bright, who had been nearby strolling through sports and social media. What happened next was beyond anything we could have prepared for.

In an instant, Mom's body went limp. Her face lost color, and she collapsed onto the ground in front of us, blacking out completely. She was unconscious, her breathing shallow and erratic. A wave of panic washed over me. I had studied biology with genuine doses of some courses similar to human biology, I had learned the signs of medical distress, but in that moment, I felt completely powerless. I could barely comprehend what was happening, let alone what to do next. Without hesitation, I instructed Bright to keep her company, hurried to the roadside, and walked in front of a moving cab and demanded the driver to stop. It was a newfound courage almost like the recent scene of President Trump pumping his fist in the air after getting shot in Butler, Pennsylvania.

In a mob of uninvited people, we lifted her into a nearby car, praying that somehow, we could get her to a hospital in time. Our town, like so many others in Ghana, had a public hospital that was chronically underfunded and often overcrowded, with the staff overwhelmed by a constant flow of patients. When we arrived, it was exactly what we feared—the doors to the public hospital were closed, the staff absent, and the facilities a chaotic mess. There was no one there who could provide the help Mom desperately needed.

With our options dwindling, we quickly

decided to take her to the nearest private hospital, hoping against hope that it would have the necessary resources and care. The journey there was long and agonizing. The roads, often unpaved and filled with potholes, made the already difficult trip even more harrowing. Every jolt and bump in the road made me wonder if we were losing precious time. My thoughts raced—would we get there in time? Could they help her? When we finally reached the private hospital, my relief was short-lived.

The facility, though better equipped than the public hospital, still faced its own limitations. The medical team sprang into action, but the situation was dire. The lack of advanced equipment, the shortage of medical professionals, and the overwhelming number of emergencies they were already managing made it clear that we were still facing significant challenges. Despite their best efforts, the reality of Ghana's healthcare system, and many others across the continent strained and under-resourced-was palpable.

I found myself caught between my train of thoughts of the cathartic systemic failure of the hospital's current state, the place I was born, and the incorrigible display of pure incompetent performance of a group of clinicians at a different infirmary that took my brother Kingsley away from us.

I was extremely vexed at the course of action

where a simple family evening would quickly spiral into a quandary of a situation. It was a moment of profound fear, frustration, and helplessness, accentuating the glaring gaps in healthcare coverage and the desperate need for improvements in medical infrastructure and safety programs. "Not today, not again!" I muttered.

Pharmaceutical companies have long been seen as champions of health, playing an instrumental role in shaping the medical landscape of the 20th century. Their contributions, especially in the mid-20th century, were nothing short of transformative. I often marvel at the intricate layers of history shared by my father—stories that weave together the global and the personal, the monumental and the intimate.

Among his most compelling tales are those chronicling humanity's triumphs against the Spanish flu pandemic of 1918, a catastrophic scourge that left no corner of the world untouched. His recounting is not merely a recitation of events but a testament to resilience—a vivid portrait of an era that demanded extraordinary resolve in the face of unprecedented loss.

Dad would most times get in the rumbles of other tales, like the chronicles of Nigeria's own metamorphosis, as seen through the lens of Fela Kuti, the irrepressible pop icon and political agitator. Fela's defiant melodies and unapologetic activism echoed through a nation in transition, as Nigeria grappled with the audacious project of shifting its capital from Lagos to Abuja. I would watch my dad, be on his feet as he gestures the dance of Fela Kuti song's *"International Thief Thief (I.T.T)"* with so much joy and the energy of an old soldier.

He would proceed to talk about the roles almost all of African youth at the time, moved afoot and few on cars to Nigeria in such of good living standard; and the struggles that this relocation will encounter a clash of tradition, aspiration, and the inevitable inertia of change.

The exact causes of the flu virus were not understood at the time. The concerted efforts of scientists, researchers, and pharmaceutical pioneers led to rapid advancements in vaccine development and public health measures. The ability to tackle the Spanish flu was just the beginning of the pharmaceutical industry's role in shaping modern medicine. Over the years, pharmaceutical companies worked tirelessly to develop life-saving drugs, vaccines, and therapies that have saved millions of lives.

The 1940s and 1950s saw the advent of penicillin and other antibiotics, which turned the tide against bacterial infections that had once been rampant, often fatal. These medicines revolutionized the treatment of diseases like tuberculosis, pneumonia, and many other bacterial infections, improving the overall quality of life for countless individuals. Big pharma as popularly known were lauded for their scientific ingenuity and their commitment to public health. Their contributions to eradicating or controlling deadly diseases such as smallpox, polio, and diphtheria were monumental.

These successes not only elevated the standing of Big Pharma but also cultivated a sense of trust and admiration for the industry. The narrative surrounding the pharmaceutical industry in the mid-20th century was one of progress, health, and the promise of a healthier tomorrow. The world was moving closer to an ideal in which previously untreatable diseases were vanquished, and life expectancy rose steadily. The 1960s and 1970s were marked by a wave of pharmaceutical breakthroughs. It was during this period that some of the most iconic medications of modern medicine were introduced. Drugs like insulin, life-saving vaccines, and treatments for chronic conditions began to be refined and made more widely available, further bolstering the global health landscape. In the context of the medical and scientific community, the pharmaceutical industry was viewed as a beacon of hope—a force that brought new hope to the sick and suffering. The development of modern antihistamines, improved cancer therapies, and the birth control pill revolutionized not only medicine but also society at large. Big Pharma, through the discovery of new treatments and cures, became the cornerstone of progress.

In many ways, these decades were a golden era for the industry, as it seemed that every new year brought with it the promise of a new miracle drug. This period of innovation laid the foundation for much of the modern healthcare system, with pharmaceutical companies positioned at the forefront of medical advancement.

However, as the decades progressed, and people like Dr. Anthony Fauci, Stefano Pessina etc., a subtle shift began to occur in the philosophy driving the pharmaceutical industry. The earlier years were characterized by a focus on curing diseases and improving the human condition, the later decades saw a gradual transition towards a more profit-driven model. The promises of universal access to life-saving drugs and treatments slowly began to erode as the global pharmaceutical giants expanded.

The turning point was particularly evident in the 1980s and 1990s when pharmaceutical companies increasingly focused on the creation of drugs designed not to cure, but to manage chronic conditions.

The rise of medications for long-term diseases like hypertension, diabetes, and high cholesterol ushered in a new era of "lifetime customers." If you have journeyed this far through the pages of this book, you'll recognize that my purpose is rooted in the things I have witnessed firsthand— the realities that have shaped my understanding of the world. These are not abstract musings or distant observations; they are the raw truths of life unfolding around me.

My mother's life is a searing indictment of a healthcare system that prioritizes profit over humanity. After undergoing a caesarean section to deliver her last child—my only sister, Gladys —she was sentenced to a lifetime of dependency on daily medication to manage unrelenting stomach pain. My sister, now in her early twenties and navigating the Sherlock Holmes of a public university, where she serves as the governor of her class; imagine the pennies spent on medications as these predatory systems have exploited from my mom and families like ours. But the story doesn't end there.

In a family of eight, living amidst the precarities of African desolated life, my mother's medical plight is just one strand in a larger web of vulnerabilities. Factor in the pervasive spread of diseases like malaria—still rampant despite being largely preventable—and the additional burdens of airborne and waterborne illnesses that often sweep through entire households. The problem compounds further when considering the environmental realities: nearby families, many of them reliant on open streams and rivers for their water sources, even to the extent of sharing those spaces with grazing farmland cattle. It's a system that perpetuates cycles of illness, poverty, and pharmaceutical dependency.

Consider the cumulative profits derived from just one individual like my mother. Multiply that by millions across the continent Africa and the Middle East who faces similar or worse conditions, and a troubling picture emerges, the chainsaw healthcare industry thrives not by curing, but by managing.

These profits, drawn from suffering, reveal a harsh reality: for many global health systems and corporations, the patients, like my mother or the dismembered grandfather of a friend of mine after his tour in Iraq is less a person and more a perpetual revenue stream. My mom had to think about simple meal deal for her kids plus swallow tablets as survival mode for her connective tissues and organs, her pain classified as an opportunity by a dude in a black monk tattered shoe, navy suit with red tie, who would take Bolognese potatoes au gratin, chocolate mousse with almonds and berries for dinner, and only worry about keeping up with his millions.

Symptoms are managed over time. The men and women in the consulting rooms, with laboratory white coats hanging around their seats, mimeographs of degrees mounted on walls, and stethoscopes around their necks have approved this ultra irrelevance and insanity. It's as if they have, what I call a BPM, the "Big Pharma Mandate" to get the hospital beds occupied at all times, hundreds of thousands of others in the lobbies and the sanatorium emergencies inhabited by human beings as if they have now developed prokaryotic genotypic traits with no nucleus for their existentialism.

Throughout college, I shared my journey with a diverse group of roommates who became not only everyday companions but inseparable part of my campus life. Bright, the anchor of our humor, could stabilize even the most chaotic moments with a quick joke. Then there was Miccah, the "godfather" of gaming, who now aspires to helm a company as its CEO. Stephen was the Korean movie enthusiast, while David, the preacher among us, has since forged a career as an engineer in North Carolina. Kingsley, with his larger-than-life persona, was the Arnold Schwarzenegger of our time—a force to be reckoned with.

Although Linda was not a roommate—as such an arrangement with ladies was naturally impractical—she was an indispensable part of my final college experience. She exuded the glamour and grace of Wallis Simpson, offering a constant luminous source of positivism and dynamism in every interaction. King Edward

VIII, of Great Britain would not mind renouncing the throne for her.

Then there was Victoria, the Londoner, whose eloquence and intellectual prowess continually pushed me to aim for greater heights. Our conversations lacked formal structure or premeditated direction; they simply began, unfolding effortlessly like a spontaneous podcast—teeming with profound insights and delightfully eccentric perspectives. Were there a grade beyond distinction, it would undoubtedly belong to her—an accolade she earned at Sheffield University while navigating an exceptionally formidable personal challenge. Her fortitude is unmatched; she is as resolute and indomitable as Malala Yousafzai.

Enoch, similarly, was not a flatmate. He was a frequent companion in spirited conversations. A natural debater and relentless questioner of established norms, he stood out as an intellectual force. Today, he thrives as a law student at Northwestern Pritzker School of Law in Chicago, an institution he proudly calls his home of prestige. Enoch never misses an opportunity to mention his place among the elite, including his chants about civil procedure and his friendship with a United States governor who happens to be his classmate—a fact he recounts with both pride and the flair of a storytelling perks on his WhatsApp channel.

Among this remarkable group, one bond

shone brightest: my friendship with Desmond Yankey. Desmond was a beacon of brilliance, standing out as one of the sharpest minds in his class. He was my longest roommate, sharing the same space for four consecutive semesters, and in that time, he revealed himself as the epitome of cool and charm. His towering frame, coupled with a Snoop Dogg-like swagger, gave him a magnetic presence, while his intellect and easy charisma brought life to every room he entered. Desmond was not merely admired; he was unforgettable, a figure who's very being seemed destined for greatness. But life, in its unrelenting capriciousness, charted a cruel course.

After college, as we embarked on the long and hopeful journeys toward realizing our aspirations, tragedy intervened. Desmond lived with the pain and the silent burden of sickle cell anemia, succumbed to his illness. His steadfast adherence to treatment and the hope kindled by modern medicine were only a trap. He fell victim to a healthcare system that prioritizes profit over compassion. His untimely passing was a shattering blow, extinguishing a light of immense promise and leaving his dreams to languish, unfulfilled, in the barren expanse of what could have been.

The pundits do not argue these lines anymore.

They are afraid to slice and dice this fatality. Fault-finders have long ceased to challenge these truths; do so now, and you'll be silenced —made redundant, sued into submission, and possibly blacklisted from the workforce entirely. The bold statements that this way of healing modernization does not only place a heavy financial burden on patients, many of whom were forced to spend a significant portion of their incomes on ongoing treatment but also falsifies the pledges and oaths taken before office assumption in the 21st century. The exorbitant prices of life-saving medications, particularly in developed nations like the United States and Germany, has sparked widespread public outrage.

Patients are faced with the harsh reality that essential drugs-such as those for cancer, heart disease, and rare diseases-are priced at levels that were often unaffordable even for the rich. In other words, only the extremely wealthy have the right to a healthy life. The industry's priorities appeared to be increasingly focused on maximizing revenue streams rather than ensuring affordable access to treatment. The short, medium and long-term consequences of these practices have devastated communities across the globe, particularly in countries with less stringent regulations and poor health care reform. What happened to the commitments to public health and public safety and their stoicism positions as responsible and trusted institutions?

Communal parking lots and many offices were now open to welcome people once again. The pandemic, in the end, did not sweep mankind off the planet. Some of the wealthiest elderly individuals were given a second chance to amend their wills and legal documents. European dogs could finally bask in the sun and enjoy the green grass, whether walked by professional dog walkers or their stay-at-home owners. Meanwhile, African dogs continued to live freely, enjoying their "bill of rights" to roam without fear of witch hunts.

Bedmakers could finally free their beds from wrinkles in the morning and return to them in grand style in the evening. Security officers at the banks were relieved from their duties of enforcing social distancing, which had been imposed by renowned health leaders like Dr. Anthony Fauci, even though he would later clarify that it was unrelated to the virus. Headscarf vendors at local transport stations and market areas began setting up their wares, and the lively early morning scene unfolded before me like a ritual of survival—my mom was one of them. Most of these vendors were mothers with mouths to feed. She had a table and was stationed there, with customers coming to her for instant transactions. She also had human carriers that would come to her to negotiate buy and sell clauses.

The first light of dawn, after President Akuffo Addo of Ghana had publicly announced to reopen the universities and major capitalist corporations, paying expository surveillance to the discoveries and update mandate of the World Health organization, crept over the clustered overhead plywood covering of our home, soft and muted, as if it too was adjusting to the world emerging from darkness. I stood in the doorway of my modest room, the early light casting shadows over walls worn by time and the hands of generations past.

Outside, the air hung with the scent of morning fires and distant car horns, the city waking to a tentative new rhythm after a year like no other. It was January 2021; I was days away from taking up a position that could change my life - a teaching assistant role at the famous medical school of my undergraduate university. It was a rare and coveted opportunity that seemed like a crack of light in the dark tunnel that had been my journey through academic studies. It was uncommon and unusual for students to blend departments. It's like I went from studying the flight of cells to trying to help students *land* their medical knowledge without crashing!

Not much was happening around the world this same time except perhaps in the Shanghai city of China where many industries were still running. Public squares in Madrid, Paris, and New York had emptied, while community hospitals overflowed as the pandemic redefined normal. Alberto Fernandez and his Argentine machine had been in lockdown for over 200 days, the longest continuous quarantine globally, yet cases remained high, and their economy was reeling. Vaccines were promised, yet far away from Africa the resources required to roll them out at scale were in short supply.

Ghana, like many nations on the continent, had limited doses, mostly designated for healthcare workers and the elderly, with little left for young professionals like me, my friends and the professors, I would be assisting. The resilience of communities meant that lockdowns were less common, for most could not afford to halt their daily work. The United Kingdom and the West had policies that supported working from home, most Africans had no such option. Survival itself demanded presence, hustle, and a reason. Being a teaching assistant in the medical field, microbiology department was incredibly challenging. Training over a thousand students while marking more than 200 scripts felt like an unrelenting task.

The sheer volume of work required constant attention and energy. Each script or assignment needed to be thoroughly reviewed, with careful feedback given to help students advance their goals. Managing this load with my colleagues, alongside the responsibility of teaching and mentoring, was a continuous balancing act. through complex materials, all in a fast-paced environment, often felt overwhelming but fun.

I could imagine the highest form of sacrifice, and the decision points that were made to leave something behind, so that me and the students could aim at something worth becoming and that upward spiraling process of transformation to climb the ladder of human kindness. It was an experience that pushed my limits and deepened my understanding of both the subject matter, the importance of effective education, and the pool of infinite possibilities that awaited these students after their training.

Beneath the joy of remembrance and thankfulness I received from most of these students after completing their six-year journey, and some even four years, for the modest part of work I did to assist them, was a looming uncertainty that awaited them. This uncertainty became apparent the moment I began to shed light on the darker thoughts and embark on the sacrificial adventure of writing this book.

I could have chosen to do something else more entertaining—and believe me, there are plenty of options. Yet, this was the harsh truth: every year, medical schools across major institutions

in the country, and even the continent, produce hundreds of graduates—young men and women who have spent seven grueling years mastering the art and science of healing—without a lever to lean on for postings to hospitals, clinics, or health facilities.

I had witnessed many who had walked the same path before me, long before I began my college education in 2016. Meanwhile, countless others would still be struggling to find stable employment by the time I graduated in 2020. It was a fate no one would wish for—nor would any parent want for their children—after leaving the comfort of home, facing the terror and triumphs of medical school, only to emerge with a degree that ultimately led to nothing of substance or meaning in the grand scheme of things. The federal government had no answers, and many of these ambitious students, unwilling to see their dreams shattered, would begin seeking scholarships abroad. This only raised concerns about the growing exodus of intellectuals from their home countries across Africa.

◆ ◆ ◆

The healthcare system of the Great Britain is overwhelmed by preventable diseases, highlighting the need for a shift toward healthier living and proactive care. For the nation's health to improve, a cultural shift emphasizing diet, exercise, and mental well-being is essential. This growing public health challenge calls for a more comprehensive approach to prevent and address the root causes of these widespread health issues. The causes of this trend are as multifaceted as they are disconcerting. Younger generations in the UK are increasingly living with the cumulative consequences of poor lifestyle choices, excessive stress, and unhealthy diets.

The consumption of highly processed foods, packed with sugar, salt, and fats, has risen to epidemic proportions, while physical inactivity is now a staple of daily life for too many. These factors, in tandem with high rates of mental health issues—anxiety, depression, and chronic stress—serve as a perfect storm for conditions like hypertension, obesity, and diabetes. All of these are well-established risk factors for strokes, yet their growing prevalence in younger populations is a signal that these health crises are being ignored or inadequately addressed. I take personal and room hygiene seriously, ensuring all surfaces, including screens, are cleaned meticulously week in and week out.

However, in recent years, there has been a noticeable decline in hygiene standards at poolside areas and other public spheres, I have witnessed guests flouting hygiene protocols—spilling food and drinks, skipping pre-swim showers, or leaving litter scattered around.

Such behaviors have not only compromised the environment but also heighten the risk of spreading germs and bacteria, endangering everyone's health. Adding to the issue, poorly maintained poolside restrooms with inadequate supplies discourage proper handwashing and foster unhygienic practices.

Whenever I travel to stay at a five-star hotel, as I did couple months ago to London for a paramount program, I have a routine: first I check to see whether the showers are running in the washroom as I don't want to wake up to any surprises the following morning. I verify that windows are not broken and there are no locked cabinets in the room. I imagine there are no hidden security cameras. No blondie hairlines left in sheets or the bathroom floor and if the heater is activated—these are essentials before I even glance at the seating arrangements.

I recently stayed in Leeds, and the hotel I booked did not live up to its price. Upon entering, I was immediately disappointed. I found used pads in the drawers, hairlines on the bedspread, remnants of a boiled egg in the kettle, oil and a handkerchief in the microwave, and an overwhelming smell of weed throughout the room. This hotel was marketed as an "epic spot" in the city, but I regretted my decision the moment I walked in. The bin was placed right outside, and it was clear that attention to cleanliness and detail was sorely lacking.

I understand that the Department for Business and Trade (DBT) plays a role in supporting the broader hospitality and tourism sectors, primarily focusing on growth and competition rather than directly overseeing hotel subpar standards or inflated pricing and poor services. However, they can still ensure that essential safety regulations are implemented and maintained. It's part of their responsibilities.

Common hygiene in hotel rooms is a critical concern, and while many establishments pride themselves on cleanliness, there's often room for improvement. Surfaces are typically wiped down, thorough disinfection of high-touch areas like remote controls, light switches, and doorknobs are sometimes overlooked. Bed linens are usually changed, but less obvious areas— such as carpets, curtains, and hidden corners —may not receive the attention they need, leading to the accumulation of dust, allergens, and bacteria. In an effort to manage costs, some hotels have streamlined housekeeping services, potentially rushing cleaning routines and compromising overall hygiene standards. You will enter a hotel and go back to your place with a legion of jetlag bacteria without any referendum for permission.

Care homes, which were once designed to house and care for the elderly, are now being forced to accommodate a new demographic —young people with chronic, often complex, medical needs. These young stroke victims, who may require specialized neurological care, physical therapy, and long-term rehabilitation, are increasingly finding themselves in environments ill-equipped to support their specific needs. The inability to prevent these stroke and cancer in younger individuals speak to a greater societal malaise-a failure to prioritize prevention and wellness over the treatment of chronic, preventable diseases. It is not simply a failure of the healthcare system; it is a failure of societal values, of a nation that has neglected to instill the importance of healthy living in its younger generations.

The increasing use of puberty blockers in the context of gender dysphoria has sparked significant debate in many communities. Some people, especially in urban centers, passionately defend the use of puberty blockers, viewing them as an essential medical intervention that allows young people to explore their gender identity in a safe, supported way. Proponents argue that the ability to pause puberty provides valuable time for children to better understand themselves and make informed decisions about their gender identity, without the irreversible physical changes that could lead to regret later in life.

This is not a conspiracy; this is sheer madness and wickedness on vulnerable people around gender identity and the medicalization of gender dysphoria, raising complex ethical questions about autonomy, the role of parents in medical decisions, and the long-term impacts on the health and well-being of young people. This is the irreversible truth: puberty blockers are a horrific crime against children and those who push them are criminals.

This is what happens when civilization is crushed by the industrial drug companies and their insurance complexes, who have engaged in deception, misinformation and disinformation when it comes to Public Health. People are no longer protected from harmful pollutants, chemicals, pesticides, pharmaceutical products, and food additives that have contributed to the overwhelming health crises in the world. In regions equipped with satellite technology and advanced cloud-based record-keeping, statistics are transparent and easily accessible.

How about the villages stretching from Tagab to Tehran to Tamale, where such infrastructure remains scarce? How do we tabulate the proliferation of expensive, symptom-managing drugs and a better health reform measures for the health of both the current and future generations? Well, good luck with that, said the Big Pharma Mandateers. Until the BPM reorient itself towards a more ethical, patient-centered model that values cures and prevention over endless treatment cycles, nine in ten future kids will be born disfigured with inevitable infirmary trips.

CHAPTER SEVEN:

THE ALLURE OF
TIMELESS WARS

*"What causes wars and what causes
fighting among you?
Is it not your passions that are at
war in your members?
You desire and do not have; so, you kill.
And you covet and cannot obtain;
so, you fight and wage war.
You do not have,
because you do not ask."*
James 4:1-2

I have not been to war. I have no gun or gunnies. I have not served in the Ghana Armed Forces or the British Navy. I have no combat experience or tours to Afghanistan or the Middle East under my belt. Neither have I pulled a person from a burning vehicle; as a matter of fact, I would be the first person to bolt or evacuate from such premises.

I have not guarded terrorist from Guantanamo Bay like the incoming Secretary of Defense, of the Trump administration of the United States of America, Pete Hegseth. The closest I have been to blood has been sustaining an injury during childhood or taking blood samples of patients thumb for malaria tests in an internship programme or watching John Wick be in his elements.

I have no credentials to make any claim or have an opinion about wars or proxy wars. But I do know how a punch in the face by a disagreeable foe mutilates. I received a public primary school education, where I carried a black backpack and wore a khaki uniform with brown shorts, always neatly pressed and tidy. I was smart, diligent but unassuming. I could tie my own shoelaces, zip up my pants, and wash my hands without being told. I earned the chance to ride a bike to school by my dad as long as I stayed in the top percentile of my class at all times. My classrooms were filled with desks, blackboards with white chalks, and learning essentials like federal text books, registration documents and never an iPad or a Wi-Fi or locker rooms.

Pupil teachers were always tasked with not only delivering lessons to large groups of students but also ensuring that noise pollution was well controlled. The hallways were vivacious and dynamic with students from different cultures and creeds during break moments, vibrating with the sounds of playing pupils: from the boys who have renamed a table tennis ball as football and kicking it on the pitch alongside stones, to the girls playing netballs as their secret admirers stood by to cheer them on, to the nerds still stuck to their desk thinking about how to send a giant water bottle filled with oxygen to planet Mars, to those playing police and thief in the lobbies and bushes of the school, a popular game where one group gets chased and beaten by the other group. It was molesting. It was juvenile. But we were just kids, and those game periods were, at times, the most motivating part of the day.

They gave us something to look forward to - a break from the classroom, where we could run, play, and swim in the adrenaline and sweat of competition. As I boosted through the grades, the contiguity and camaraderie of those earlier years began to go on a downward spiral on some days into something I had taken for granted. I progressed and left old classrooms behind. In each advanced stage or grade, there were students who had repeated the year due to poor cumulative academic performances.

These individuals, often significantly larger and older than me, did not seem to possess a greater understanding of the material, affirming my father's teachings that knowledge has no correlation with age or status but hard work and discipline. Their size and age seemed to give them a sense of entitlement. They were mostly the back seated group. I chose to be a forward desk user.

I was advised early on by my salient parents that a seat at the men's table starts from a seat in the classroom, particularly and perennially in the front beaches; as an airline pilot with a straightforward worldview as he responds to changing weather turbulence, ensuring the flight stays on course and follows aviation regulations and not the backseats, like a comedian who is entirely mixed up in his first stand up show of 20,000 audiences at Madison Square Garden. I held onto these truths. The only downside to sitting in the front seat was that I became the first to receive the full force of the teacher's aggressive reprimands.

I also faced the consequence of the chalkboard's remnants—those delicate, ethereal particles of wiped chalk that floated in the air and inevitably settled on and around me. The soft, powdery dust lingered in the classroom, a quiet trace of the lessons that had once been written, now erased but still present in the air I breathed. I was a small, skinny kid with a big head. Hence, that would be the license for these bad boys, an approval for action. I was easily bullied left, right, center, sometimes even in my dreams. I was not tormented alongside those who knew how to do their assignments, asked stupid questions and excelled academically. It became a struggle reminiscent of the David and Goliath story—where intellect and diligence were met with truculence and insecurity.

The bullying was subtle at first—a passing remark here, a whispered affront there. But soon it escalated, as if each comment, each shove in the hallway, was a meagre skirmish in a larger, unseen war. The classroom, once a place of learning, became a battlefield where the proxy wars of jealousy, insecurity, and power played out in the form of taunts and cruel jokes. It was a war waged not with weapons, but with words, punches, and social maneuvers, each attack was a commanding victory for these adversaries to hit harder or move to the next victim. It was an ongoing challenge, and more often than not, the bullies were reported to the authorities.

However, the true difficulty lay in the fact that even when a teacher intervened and took action to put an end to the harassment, the resolution was short-lived and proved fleeting. After school, they would fatefully be waiting, ready to resume their calling without consequence. Years later, I would emerge from this ordeal with a newfound strength, armed with a sense of self-preservation and resilience.

I formulated a strategy of strike first but heavily, relied on the speed of my bike and oftentimes on the athleticism of my legs, channeling the energy of a sprinter like Usain Bolt, ready to outpace any pursuers and leave my tormentors far behind. I didn't realize it at first, but things begin to take on meaning as time passes, the bullying in those corridors was the microcosm of something much broader about human existentialism; a transmogrified model of how nations engaged in proxy wars.

Those back benches always fought for dominance or for fulfillment in the classroom as they had nothing else to boast of or to utilize to win the beautiful ladies over. I assumed the role of a small nation caught between the larger powers of envy and fear. The sacred place of teaching and learning became a Waterloo battleground where others fought for control over my sense of alacrity and dignity. It wasn't just about me, it was about what I represented: the threat of someone who had the potential to rise above, to be different, to outshine my formal self. The classroom, in its way, mirrored the tensions between nations in the world today, where the strongest are often the ones who bore the brunt of the war, the ones who stood alone against overwhelming forces.

Now I look back and see the schoolyard bullying not as isolated acts of cruelty, but as ordinate orchestration of the weak or envious men of our world. The wars fought silently between those who seek power and those who refuse to be crushed by it. The wars of those who just want to analyze their tyrannical war machines at refugee hospitals in Gaza or embark on missile tests deregulations in South Korea after assembling them in the Garden of Kim Jong Un's Eden.

My dad dreamed of joining the military, captivated by the ideals of discipline, honor, and valor. His ambition was thwarted by my grandfather, who refused to let him enlist. This decision wasn't born out of doubt in my dad's courage or capability —qualities he already possessed in abundance. Instead, it stemmed from a deep-seated fear, rooted in my grandfather's own complicated life. My grandfather, having married multiple wives and later divorcing my grandmother without ensuring her stability or security for their children, likely foresaw the possibility of his son's resentment. He feared what military training might add to my dad's natural resolve —strength that could challenge his authority and choices. It was an act of self-preservation disguised as paternal concern.

Years ahead, my dad speculatively uncovered the real reason for his dashed dream, it cut him deeply. However, instead of succumbing to bitterness, he channeled his energy into physical discipline, training with the intensity of a kickboxer. He pushed himself relentlessly, as though preparing for battles he would never fight. Though the military remained beyond his reach, his life reflected the heart of a warrior —tenacious, resilient, and unyielding in the face of life's challenges. My father approached parenthood with the precision and discipline of a military commander, instilling in us the virtues of sacrifice, responsibility, and an unwavering commitment to moral integrity.

His guidance was deliberate and structured, ensuring that my siblings and I—including my youngest sister—were aligned on a path rooted in righteousness and ethical clarity. He didn't merely preach values; he lived them, modeling the importance of accountability and selflessness in every aspect of his life. Through his actions, we learned to prioritize not just personal success but also the well-being of those around us as well as full support to go after our dreams.

At university, I joined debate societies, got into constructive conversations in the study rooms or rooftops in the middle of the night, mostly gravitated toward those with sharper intellects and more incisive arguments than my own. We delved into weighty topics, one of which often centered on the essence of civilian leadership in times of crisis.

Figures like Volodymyr Zelensky frequently became a focal point, after he took the oath of office in may 2019, his transformation from comedian to wartime president a compelling study in the unexpected demands of leadership. Zelensky's unyielding resolve to confront Vladimir Putin's military aggression—despite the uneven odds of Ukraine's forces, even with NATO's support (notably excluding direct involvement by the United States)—highlights the tension between symbolism and strategy in leadership and character.

His stance encapsulates the enduring power of civilian resolve, even against the might of a global power like Russia. I've often pondered Zelensky's gamble, questioning whether his insistence on victory is a reflection of courageous defiance or a calculated strategy to rally not just his nation but the world for his self-centered gains.

His leadership underscores a profound paradox: civilian leaders in such conflicts are compelled to balance the moral imperatives of resistance with the harsh pragmatism of geopolitics. After months of relentless conflict, it's hard to ignore the growing suspicion that Volodymyr Zelensky's priority may not be the well-being of his people, but rather the perpetuation of the war itself. His bunker hidden courage and resolve have earned him international acclaim particularly after his "I need ammunition not a ride" speech went viral on the internet and cable news networks across the world. Time magazine praised him as the Person of the Year 2022. It appears like the mounting death toll and destruction within Ukraine suggest a different story.

I am not a critic of Ukraine and have no relative residing there, at least not that I know of, however by prolonging the war, Zelensky risks the lives of his citizens in pursuit of a victory that feels increasingly elusive, all while appearing more focused on garnering international aid and bolstering his own position than ending the suffering. He triggered martial law to stay in power. Russia had free and fair elections in March. He puts on military-style t-shirts, he delivers frequent videos on X to appeal to international alliances, requesting financial support to sustain his nation's war effort. Allegations have surfaced suggesting that some of these funds are diverted toward personal luxuries, such as customizing expensive cars for his wife.

The question now is whether his leadership reflects genuine concern for Ukraine's future, or if personal and political motives are clouding the moral imperative to protect his people. It is both alarming and absurd for children under eighteen in cities like Poznan or Porto Novo to be exposed to graphic images of the horrific massacres occurring in Ukraine. This exposure, often via media outlets, strips away the innocence of youth, leaving them to process violence and destruction that are worlds apart from their daily experiences.

The psychological impact on these young minds is profound, as they are introduced to the stark realities of war without the maturity or context to fully understand it. Meanwhile, Western governments, particularly in the U.S. and the EU, continue to pour vast sums of money and military support into Ukraine's defense against giant Russia, only to cause more displacement of families to be refugees and homeless in cities like Berlin and Birmingham.

President Zelensky's firm stance against brokering a deal with Vladimir Putin, coupled with a refusal to seek diplomatic resolution is despicable, dangerous and divisive. This is a senseless war. I want my friends rebranded as trooped; either it was their will or not, in the British Military like Paul, a selfless man who doubles up his duties in the house of God and Canadian Airforce like Michael to stay alive and comeback home. It would matter a lot more than for them to be reduced to a mere statistic. The true cost of such avertible deaths cannot be captured in a two-hour Remembrance Day event as a commemoration, no matter how well-intentioned.

In his famous 2004 speech, Senator Barack Obama recounted that, war may not be the best option and it should never be the first option. That speech amongst other things will make him the flag bearer for the Democratic ticket and also two terms as president. Kids born in 2008 will grow up knowing a black man as the President of the United States, for eight years, however now those remarks and such important factions have been shelved and forgotten. He might not have been the expert on foreign policies or America First approach like President Donald Trump but he sure had some great successes for his country and the world including the elimination of Usama Bin Laden, the stop of Ebola and the leap from the Great Recession.

This passage is about the rhetoric: and how things turned out in the conscientious story of Cain and Abel that unfolded in the Garden of Eden. If you are familiar with the story of Cain and Abel, you will recall that Cain's tragic decision to resolve his frustration through violence marked the beginning of humanity's history of fratricide —a decision rooted in jealousy and a refusal to confront his own shortcomings. For those less acquainted, revisiting this biblical account is a sobering reflection on human nature and the consequences of unchecked emotions and misrepresentations of weak leaders in the modern world. Cain, aggrieved by God's favoring of Abel's offering, could have chosen dialogue or introspection to address his feelings of rejection. Instead, he turned to violence, lashing out at the very person who represented his grievance.

Federal governments and global institutional bodies often prioritize political or economic agendas over the lives of civilians. This is evident in the ongoing conflicts in Yemen or Syria or South Sudan where international powers often turn a blind eye to humanitarian crises, focusing instead on strategic interests. Barack Obama's vision of unity stands as a direct rebuttal to Cain's isolating mindset, advocating instead for the recognition of shared humanity, collective attention to what matters.

Starting a conversation, whether with a beautiful stranger or a potential mentor, has never been an issue, I thrive in that forte when I want to be.

Though, I often find myself torn between eagerness and hesitation, unsure of how to bridge the gap. My ambivalence stems from a desire to make meaningful connections while being apprehensive of the possibility of saying too much—or too little. I am inclined toward lucid, engaging exchanges, especially with individuals whose intellect or insights captivate me. These conversations, however, tend to be few and far between, as I am selective in my engagement. My preference is to discuss ideas and perspectives that expand my understanding of the world—a retrospection of my need to stay informed and become intellectually stimulated.

From the vantage of my student accommodation window, the world outside feels frozen and baltic in a deep, unyielding grip. The temperature hovers at a biting -2°C, and the chill is almost palpable, hanging in the air like an uninvited guest. The street below appears still, almost as if suspended in time, the few passersby moving briskly, their breaths misting in the air before dissipating in the cold, like fleeting traces of warmth. It was my first December in Great Britain, I begun to rethink my choices of considering this over an average of room temperature or 298K in Africa. The Northern Hemisphere of the UK is equipped with unstable weather conditions more than down South, the kind where the sky is a uniform slate of clouds and within moments becomes thick with the promise of more rain or possibly snow.

I wished for a snow to happen and it did, it was marvelous in the eyes but monstrous being in it. I walked through the corridor of my student accommodation to the shared kitchen space. The aisle was decorated with twinkling fairy lights draped along the walls, casting a gentle shimmer that danced in the dim light. Christmas festive wreaths with red ribbons adorn the doors, and small garlands of holly and pine stretch across the edges. At the far end, a small, decorated Christmas tree stands in a corner, its ornaments reflecting the fulgurating lights.

The entire space feels inviting and joyful, a warm contrast to the cold winter air outside. I encountered a microcosm of a global conflict encapsulated in the anguish and resolve of a young woman from Taiwan, who had also come to study. She stood across from me, her expression a blend of exhaustion and determination, as she unpacked the emotional toll of Taiwan's precarious relationship with China.

What began as a brief errand to retrieve an oat milk from the fridge, and spotted her making dinner and asked about how her day has been turned to a 90 minutes sobering marathon of history, politics, and personal anguish. Her sentiments were heavy with both sorrow and anger, her tone oscillating between defiance and vulnerability. She spoke with the precision of someone who had thought deeply about the intricate, often painful, narrative of her homeland. Raised in Taiwan, she described the island as a vibrant democracy under the constant shadow of Beijing's claims—a place where resilience is a daily necessity and identity is a battleground.

According to her, Taiwan's history came alive, from its indigenous roots and colonial legacies to its transformation into a democratic stronghold in East Asia. She lamented the fabrications woven into international discourse, narratives that obscure Taiwan's self-determination in favor of appeasing global powers. Her frustrated submission was not just academic—it was deeply personal. Her family remained in Taiwan, navigating the tensions of life in a contested space while she, thousands of miles away, wrestled with feelings of helplessness. Amid her despair was an unshakable resolve and not retreat. She was clear in her purpose: to succeed academically, return home, and contribute to the preservation of Taiwan's sovereignty. She spoke of a dream to protect her family and ensure their safety, her ambition fueled by the quiet urgency of a generation determined to resist the erosion of their identity.

As I left that kitchen, I found myself carrying more than just oat milk. I carried the clones of her story, a reminder that geopolitical conflicts are not distant abstractions but deeply human crises. In her voice, I heard the resilience of a people unwilling to be defined by the ambitions of others. According to her, Taiwan's struggle was far more than an ideological stance; it was a matter of survival and national identity —an unflinching testament to the strength of the individual in the face of seemingly insurmountable odds. I have never been a victim of a nation at war and I don't ever wish to be.

People like Professor Gad Saad and Secretary of States to President Nixon, Henry Kissinger exemplified the resilience of those who fled unimaginable turmoil to forge new paths in safer lands. Professor Saad was fortunate to escape the chaos of Lebanon, where sectarian violence fractured communities and uprooted countless families during the brutal civil war. The Lebanon he left behind was one where survival often meant abandoning one's home, culture, and memories for the faint hope of safety elsewhere. Similarly, Henry Kissinger's escape from Nazi Germany as a young boy underscores the harrowing choices faced by families under the shadow of genocide. Kissinger fled a regime that sought to annihilate not just individuals but an entire people, forcing him and his family to leave their lives in Fürth behind to survive.

The story of the flat mate I met in the communal kitchen, along with many others from regions plagued by conflict, reminded me of the xenophobic violence that occurred in the tragic events of 1989 in Nigeria. My father was working in Lagos during those turbulent times. I hadn't been born yet, but his stories of that period remain vivid in my mind. There was a raw, uneasy mix of passion and agony in his voice as he recounted how he narrowly escaped death at the hands of a mob. It was a chilling tale of survival, painted with flashes of humor that only hindsight can offer. As he spoke, I would imagine the faces of my parents during those moments: my father, navigating danger with a blend of courage and desperation, and my mother, left behind with three young children, living through the agony of uncertainty. Without any reliable means of communication, she had no way of knowing whether her husband was safe or if she was already a widow.

The events of 1989, known as the "Ghana Must Go" crisis, were sparked by economic and political unrest in Nigeria. The Nigerian government, under President Ibrahim Babangida, decided to expel over a million foreign nationals, with a significant number of them being Ghanaians. The decision was partly a reaction to economic strain and growing unemployment, exacerbated by the influx of migrants during the 1970s and 1980s.

What followed was a horrifying wave of violence and hostility. Many Ghanaians were forced to flee their homes, their businesses were looted and destroyed, and they faced severe physical abuse from Nigerian citizens who saw them as competitors for jobs, resources, and opportunities. This xenophobic hostility reached its peak with attacks on Ghanaian homes and businesses, largely with no legal recourse for the victims.

People who had once lived peacefully in Nigeria for years found themselves suddenly demonized, forced out, and subjected to harassment, and violence. My dad reported seeing a friend caught in an unthinkable predicament: ambushed in the middle of nowhere, a vehicle tire forced around his neck, doused in fuel, and set ablaze.

It was an act of barbarity so stark and cruel that even recounting it felt like reopening a wound. What struck me most wasn't just the brutality of the act but the silence it demanded. Explaining such an incident to the authorities wasn't an option. The police themselves compromised or too afraid to act, might just as easily inform the perpetrators, turning the whistleblower into the next victim.

Justice wasn't absent, it had been hijacked, weaponized, and rendered a tool of fear rather than protection. As a child, hearing this story left a profound mark on me. It authenticated how perilously thin the veneer of civilization can be. The boundary between order and chaos, between humanity and savagery, felt alarmingly close. The absence of justice, where fear becomes the dominant force and silence the only refuge, revealed how much societies depend on fairness and accountability for their survival. Without these cornerstones, communities collapse into an abyss where even survival carries the weight of moral compromise.

In Today's world, the prospect of a global war presents a far graver and more complex threat than in the past. Unlike the makeshift tools and untrained individuals who carried out atrocities in localized conflicts, like the amateur local warlocks with little to no education on the Obajana-Kabba Road who specialized in setting people on fire, a modern conflict would be orchestrated by some of the most brilliant minds in society, armed not with rudimentary weapons but with the destructive capabilities of advanced technologies, chemical expertise, and nuclear arsenals. The stakes are exponentially higher. A single modern weapon can obliterate entire cities, erasing in moments what humanity has painstakingly cultivated over millennia—art, culture, architecture, and the bonds of human civilization itself.

Consequential proxy wars in the 21st century is no longer fought solely on battlefields but extend to cybernetic domains, economic systems, and even the planet's ecological stability. This is a looming danger, encouraging the story of Dr. J. Robert Oppenheimer's famous statement of "now, I am become deaths, the destroyer of worlds" and the culmination of physics leading to the creation of the atomic bomb. Keir Starmer, leader of the UK Labour Party, may seek to present himself as a hydrostatic option to Winston Churchill, the towering figure of British wartime leadership. Churchill's legacy is defined by his resolve to lead Britain through the Second World War, a man whose covalent will gained instrumental feat in the defeat of Nazi Germany.

Prime Minister Starmer seems to be contending with the complexities of modern geopolitics, contemplating toward military options, including the potential use of advanced weapons like the UK's Storm Shadow missiles in Russia forgetting the primacy that President Putin was a formal *Komitet Gosudarstvennoy Bezopasnosti,* KGB who served for over 15 years, in a place; which was designated as a breeding ground for an unforgiving, secretive, and pragmatic worldview. It may appear as a mere fantasy at first until it quickly turns into a harsh reality after been ignored and capitalized by inaction.

From the rugged coastlines of Northern Ireland to the troubled phosphates of Naura to the Sandinistas of Nicaragua, it baffles me and it's increasingly disheartening to see the growing rhetoric against capitalism from leaders around the world, especially when they overlook the undeniable role it has played in shaping the modern world. From fueling the rise of skyscrapers, to the manufacturing of the marvels of global technologies, and to the achievements of space exploration, such as the

International Space Station.

These are living proofs of what free and open markets can achieve when leveraged correctly, however the students of Karl Marx and the socialist occult groups of Bernie Sanders and Kamala Harris have begun their evil crusades of waging ideological wars on capitalism without considering that it has, at its core, lifted millions out of poverty and enabled global collaboration on a scale never seen before in human history. And in doing so, they have created an environment of uncertainty, where bad decisions, not solutions, has become the norm —leading to a future that is both economically stagnant and politically irrelevant.

The Middle East have been a home for massive oil reserves, setting for the towering Burj Khalifa—the tallest building in the world and the longest-running unending most bitter rivalries on the planet. I've had the opportunity to visit Dubai, and walking through its gleaming streets, it's impossible not to marvel at the rapid development and the gleaming skyline that stretches towards the heavens. Beneath the surface of this modernity rests a long and tumultuous history.

It was during my college years that I witnessed a significant shift in the region's geopolitical landscape: President Donald Trump's administration brokered the Abraham Accords. These agreements, aimed at normalizing relations between Israel and several Arab nations, marked a historical moment in a region often defined by conflict. This wasn't merely an isolated political maneuver; it was a calculated break with history. For decades, the dominant narrative in the region had been one of perpetual conflict, where alliances formed largely along sectarian and ideological lines.

The Abraham Accords suggested that shared goals such as: combating extremism, leveraging economic opportunities, and countering Iranian influence could override these divisions. They represented a pragmatic acknowledgment that peace, however imperfect, was often more lucrative than unending war. President Trump's administration, particularly through Jared Kushner's backchannel negotiations, deserves credit for seizing on this moment. Far left radical critics of President Trump may hesitate to acknowledge it, but the accords were a significant achievement.

They were bold in their conception and groundbreaking in their execution, prompting some to suggest that Trump was and still is a worthy contender for the Nobel Peace Prize. The moment President Trump exited office in January 2020, so too did the fervor for expanding the accords. The enduring mishap of diplomacy is that it often transcends partisan lines but remains vulnerable to political whims. Whether a Republican or Democrat, conservative or liberal, crafts a peace agreement have dictated its value or future.

The Abraham Accords are an emblem of this reality. In today's polarized political landscape, it has become increasingly common for opposition parties to overturn or obstruct budgets—whether in the sedated corridors of Abuja, Nigeria, or the serene parliamentary halls of Wellington, New Zealand or the brutal dark forces in Georgia, Budgets, meant to outline priorities and allocate resources for citizens' welfare, have become Vietnam warzone for political brinkmanship.

This global pattern illustrates how governance is frequently sidetracked by partisan agendas. Instead of focusing on long-term strategies to uplift citizens, opposing parties sometimes seek to dismantle policies simply to undermine their rivals, regardless of the impact on the people. The consequences are far-reaching: stalled public projects, delayed infrastructure development, and unmet social welfare needs. Great transformational budgets are now the first victim of political gamesmanship, something that should be regarded as roadmaps for national or global progress, transcending party lines. True leadership which requires collaboration and a shared commitment to the people's prosperity is a bygone just like the Typewriter machine where ever you go. It matters more than ever which president or party signed the agreement or the important legislation.

The suffering of displaced families and the unyielding cycles of violence are blind to partisan labels. Such landmark agreements are left to languish, the human cost is staggering affirming the invaluable Michael Jackson's outcry song; "They Don't Care About Us." In my quest of making this book, at this very division, as I continue to put my conscientious thoughts and logical concerns into this episode, many of the world's most powerful leaders have convened in Brazil for the G20 Summit, 2024. A reoccurring event, a gathering that, on paper, could serve as the nexus for groundbreaking global change. They arrive on taxpayer-funded jets that emit copious amounts of carbon into the atmosphere and sit down to talk to us about climate change crises.

The spectacle has been familiar. Leaders engage in photo ops, deliver speeches brimming with lofty promises, and participate in symbolic handshakes. Some of them even have undermined the effectiveness of powerful handshakes that take place after a potent negotiation has been achieved. Young men stopped shopping for suits from Slaters and Marks & Spencer as thugs and criminals, weak and dark men often possess these on their screens. The despondent and troubling reality is that, after all the speeches, handshakes, and strategic meetings, the world's political elite will return home with little to show for their global jaunts.

The most tangible outcome of these summits often isn't a transformative deal or a new resolution to address global crises, but a series of glossy photos destined for social media feeds and office walls. These carefully curated images featuring powerful leaders posing with figures like President Xi of China or Felipe VI of Spain are then paraded as evidence of their growing influence. These fleeting moments of visibility, not taking into account their superficialities, are used to bolster their public image, signaling to constituents and rivals and escorts alike that they've made it to the top, even if the substantive issues remain untouched.

The wars raging in Eastern Europe and the Middle East will remain relentless. For the youth caught in the crossfire, their dreams will be stifled if not crushed under the umbrella of destruction. Inflation will continue to erode livelihoods and levelled homes. In the twilight of modern leadership, the truth is crystalline and glassy. We stand alone, naked and unimmunized.

I am not aiming to sound as pessimistic as Authur Schopenhauer nonetheless we are on our own with no one to place reliance on, not even our biological mothers can aid us because they are unreachable or our doctors, as both have been compromised, not that they chose to or have jettisoned us; but in view of the fact that, they have had their worlds devoured by similar trends promoted by previously held wanton leaderships.

CHAPTER EIGHT:

THE TYRANNY OF
THE MINORITY

*"When it was day, the Jews made a plot
and bound themselves by an oath neither to eat
nor drink till they had killed Paul.
There were more than forty who
made this conspiracy.
And they went to the chief priests
and elders, and said,
we have strictly bound ourselves by an
oath to taste no food till we have killed Paul.
You therefore, along with the council,
give notice now to the tribune to
bring him down to you,
as though you were going to determine
his case more exactly.
And we are ready to kill him before he comes near."*

Acts 23:12-15

T he lines between boys and girls seemed drawn with unshakable precision when I was younger. The world around me had a way of defining gender differences through explicit, sometimes unspoken, boundaries. The boys' world was defined by strength, activity, and the occasional boisterous chaos of roughhousing. In my suburban primary school, the boys' bathroom often mirrored the untamed energy that defined our adolescent years. It was less a space for hygiene and order than one for survival, where the goal was simply to get in and out without incident. The air, thick with the acrid smell of stale urine and half-hearted cleaning products, was a testament to the rawness of the space.

The floors, perpetually slippery and stained, seemed to absorb the chaos that pervaded the room. Cleaners would frequent the boys' washroom multiple times a day—often three— while the girls' restroom, though not without its own wear, might only need attention once. This disparity wasn't just about the volume of use, but also about how the space was treated. Paper towels, used and discarded with little thought, cluttered the floors, while overflowing urinals added to the disorder. The noise was an extension of the mess: loud, unrefined, and filled with the same hurried energy that defined every boy at that stage of life.

Conversations often spilled into the space, rapid and raucous, while the occasional crash or scuffle underscored the lack of discipline. My primary school may not have had the resources for top-tier educational support but it could afford for the unmistakable signs; stark and simple, in their intent and marked the boys' bathroom. Among the directives to "keep it clean" and "aim properly," there were also bold, almost cartoonish sketches designed to make one thing perfectly clear: this was a space for boys, and boys alone. Even toddlers and toddlers' carers, upon entering, could understand the crude, still effective symbols that delineated the bathroom's purpose and its users even though the school did not have a different one for vulnerable and babies.

The signs left no room for confusion—this was a domain set apart, a space where gender was both a social and physical delineation, reinforced by the bold clarity of the visual markers. The girls' bathroom, on the other hand, was an enigma—one that defied the understanding of boys. It was a domain bound by invisible rules, subtly guarded by societal expectations that separated it from our chaotic, unrestrained space. It was discussed with a quiet reverence, as though it held a dignity that we could neither touch nor fully comprehend. It was a place that sustained order, a realm marked by distinctions not only of space but of behavior, where cultural norms, unspoken but universally acknowledged, took form.

To us, it became a boundary, not just physically but ideologically, a place marked by difference, reinforced by exclusion, where access was prohibited, and curiosity was stifled by the very idea of separation. The girls' restroom wasn't just a room—it was a microcosm of the broader societal divisions that structured our understanding of gender roles, identities, underwear adjustments and delicate wedgie removals.

I was ignorant and curious, much like many young children who stand at the threshold of understanding the world. My questions about the physical and social divisions between boys and girls occupied my thoughts, and I couldn't help but wonder: What really separated us? Why were these differences so sharply defined, even in places like the school bathroom?

It wasn't until that seemingly ordinary moment when I stumbled upon a young girl taking a bath in the open that my curiosity was met with a profound revelation. I wasn't a voyeur, but a witness to something raw and human— an unintentional peek into a life I had only been taught to observe from afar. The sight was simple and earthy and it carried the magic wand of Gandalf that shifted my perception in a way no mercurial explanation or rule could debate.

I realized that the barrier that separated me and a girl, like I was advised to refrained from any girls-only space—those external, physical distinctions—were not just the surface, they were on the surface.

I recorded the clear anatomical organs visible to my eye, that are definitively correlated with chromosomes, and have been since time memorial of human history. Beneath the clothes lied a much deeper and more complex but simply expressed layer of humanity. I will later learn in introductory to natural sciences that, girls have two X chromosomes, a uterus and vagina and they are capable to reproduce offsprings. Boys have X and Y chromosome, a penis and testicles, and they are not able to give birth.

Much more knowledge would be added as I climbed the school lather including deep genetics and variation studies and compounding importance of testosterone for men and the dominant nature of oxytocin and prolactin in women. The thoughts of stating these kindergarten ideas to anyone let alone write them in a book, were never part of my imagination as to consider being ready to defend my claims in a court house.

The world today is torn between science and ideology. As humanity climbs ever higher on the ladder of technological and intellectual advancement, breaking barriers once deemed insurmountable, we also seem to be descending into an ideological quagmire. The world grows taller in knowledge and technology, constructing monumental skyscrapers and building intelligent machines capable of talking and reasoning. We stand on the precipice of what was once science fiction: artificial intelligence, genetically edited embryos, autonomous vehicles, and digital currencies. Yet, amidst these towering advancements, we are facing a bizarre regression in fundamental social structures, such as the longstanding distinctions between boys' and girls' bathrooms.

There was once a time when hurricanes were given women's names as part of a tradition, not because of any political statement, but because of the cultural norms and conventions that shaped that practice. These names, assigned without malice, were reflective of a world that understood and respected basic biological realities. The categorization of gender as male and female was not a matter for debate—it was simply a fact. Chromosomal markers, XY for men and XX for women, stood as the unwavering foundation of our understanding of sex and gender.

They provided the bedrock for societies, for science, for education, and yes, for the very design of facilities like bathrooms. Today, these foundational truths are being eroded by what can only be described as ideological zealotry. The lines between male and female are being blurred beyond recognition. This isn't a mere challenge to traditional gender roles; it is the overt denial of biological science.

In schools, workplaces, and even in judicial appointments, we see the rise of what can only be called "social atavism"—a backward-looking, ideologically driven rejection of science in favor of politically correct dogma. In this climate, the basic and self-evident truths about biology are tossed aside like irrelevant artifacts from a bygone era. It may seem an exaggeration to some, but the erosion of these biological truths' manifests in the most absurd ways. Some boys, caught up in the gender identity conversation, now wear feminine hygiene products like pads and bras as part of their new "identity"— a performance of gender that defies not just reason but reality.

These are not isolated incidents but signs of a larger movement where the very nature of sex is being replaced by a manufactured understanding of "gender," one that shifts with every social trend and emotional appeal. The traditional concept of gender as binary—male and female—has been tossed into the ideological blender.

The rise of transgender rights, in the contemporary governments which they deemed it necessary for the protection of those who identify as something other than their biological sex, has become a flashpoint for a broader cultural revolution. In the name of inclusion, we are told to accept the idea that men can become women, and women can become men, with no regard for the chromosomal and physiological differences that have existed since the dawn of humanity.

Imane Khelif is a notable Algerian boxer who made history by winning a gold medal at the 2024 Paris Olympics in the women's welterweight category, making him the first African boxer to earn an Olympic title in this sport reserved for women. Yes! You read that right, this atrocity happened just couple months ago.

Schools, once bastions of reason and education, are now the battlefields where this social war plays out. Children are told that gender is fluid and that their biological sex is nothing more than a social construct. In some cases, young boys who identify as girls are given access to girls' bathrooms, while girls who identify as boys are given similar privileges. The very concept of a safe, single-sex space is being dismantled, all in the name of equality.

This cultural movement goes beyond bathrooms and reaches into the heart of our core partialized institutions. Judicial appointments, once based on qualifications and legal expertise, are now at times being informed by a commitment to ideological representation. Social activists, far more concerned with gender quotas and identity politics, are occupying roles that once required expertise and experience.

The justice system, which was founded on the principles of fairness, equality before the law, and impartiality, is now often subjected to political manipulation. What was once a system designed to uphold the dignity and rights of individuals is now a vehicle for ideological warfare. In a political landscape marked by escalating culture wars, one curious development has surfaced in the halls of U.S. Congress: the increasing requirement for delegates to state their pronouns before making a claim or speaking in executive meetings. Republicans, having secured major wins in the last election cycle, have turned this trend into a punchline. Senator Steve Daines of Montana have cheekily replaced "she/her" with "Republican/Majority" during their pronoun introductions, especially after the GOP's success in taking control of the House, Senate, and the Presidency.

I suppose it was meant to be a tactical move—part political commentary, part cultural satire—that plays into the growing tensions between progressive efforts at inclusivity and conservative skepticism about these shifts.

There is a growing cohesion perceived as "compulsory" engagement with topics like pronouns and identity in many facets of public life. In this new reality, the very essence of amity and spirituality is under siege. Humanity's shared values—those that bind us together as a society—are being overshadowed by a relentless push to redefine human nature based on individual feelings and subjective experiences.

The results of this revolution are clear: a fractured society, where division is championed as inclusion, and where the pursuit of equality often leads to the exclusion of the very truths that hold us together. The pursuit of equality has morphed into a kind of egalitarianism that seeks not just equal rights but equal outcomes, regardless of the natural, biological differences that shape our lives. This mentality demands that we ignore science, dismissing it as an inconvenient truth. We are told that all men can become women, that all women can become men, and that the very concept of masculinity and femininity is a construct—something to be deconstructed and remade according to the whims of the moment.

As society grows increasingly complex and machinery advanced, we seem to be drifting away from the foundational truths that have historically united and propelled us forward. The principles that enabled humanity to construct thriving civilizations and achieve monumental feats—such as President JFK's audacious vision of sending a man to the moon— and the understanding of world around us are now being traded for ideologies that seek to not morally compromise but remake the world in the image of an imbecilic future, disconnected from the reality of human biological responsibilities.

The question remains: will we continue to build upward in knowledge and achievement, or will we descend into a society that has lost touch with the very foundations of reason and reality? The choice we face today is not just a political one but a moral and a sophisticated philosophical one.

Will we allow ourselves to be swept up in a tide of unreason, where the pursuit of inclusion leads us to deny the science that has shaped our understanding of the world? Or will we reclaim the virtues of logic, reason, and truth, recognizing that true equality is not achieved by ignoring the differences that make us who we are, but by embracing them with respect and understanding?

Feminism began as a clarion call for justice—a movement to level the playing field in a world where systemic inequality was the norm. It aimed to dismantle oppressive systems and create opportunities for women to thrive alongside men, not at their expense. Leaders like Rosa Parks defied prejudice to ignite transformative civil rights movements. Political pioneers like Angela Merkel and Theresa May demonstrated that women could steer nations with intelligence and strength.

As noble as these roots are, the modern landscape of feminism is increasingly marked by troubling overcorrections that risk alienating the very allies needed to achieve equity. President Ronald Reagan, with his characteristic humor, once remarked, *"The problem with our liberal friends isn't that they're ignorant; it's just that they know so much that isn't so."* I cannot help but feel this applies to elements of modern feminism. What was once a movement rooted in collaboration and empowerment has, in some quarters, become a crusade with diminishing regard for balance or reason.

Some feminists now vilify men wholesale, portraying them as obstacles to progress rather than partners in creating a just world. This shift reflects not only a loss of direction but also a fundamental misunderstanding of what equality should mean. The new tyranny is no longer at our doorstep but in our living rooms. It's increasingly common to hear narratives suggesting that men should relinquish their roles in leadership, innovation, and society at large.

This attitude not only undermines the contributions men have historically made but also ignores the mutual interdependence of the sexes in building the world we now enjoy. The wage gap narrative, while valid in some contexts, has led to caricatures of men as oppressors and women as perpetual victims. Now, some women, buoyed by rising incomes or institutional quotas, treat their partners as competitors rather than equals. This ideology has given rise to an atmosphere of antagonism, where the achievements of women are celebrated not for their merit but as weapons in a battle against men. But is this truly progress? Or is it a witch-hunt that conflates justice with revenge?

Ingenious women—scientists, educators, entrepreneurs—have always shaped society. However, reducing men to disposable footnotes in the story of human advancement does no service to equality. It creates a vacuum where collaboration should thrive. I did not have the privilege of growing up under the nurturing care of either a paternal or maternal grandmother. But my understanding of the unique strength and grace of women was shaped profoundly by the smaller, everyday examples that surrounded me.

I saw the fire and fury in the eyes of my mother, when I was ripening, who balanced the rigors of domestic life with an unyielding pursuit of better opportunities for her children. My sister, similarly driven, carved a path for herself in a field dominated by men, not by tearing others down but through sheer perseverance and talent. Beyond my immediate family, the women in my parents' neighborhood including the young girls, who by the mandatory seating arrangement of our class teacher found themselves beside me, offered similar insights. Whether they were tending to their families, pursuing their own ambitions, or simply navigating the complexities of their daily chores, they exhibited a quiet power that spoke volumes. These women didn't demand the world bow to their gender; they earned respect through their actions, peace through strength in the face of adversity.

Today, however, this flame is being redirected. Instead of using that fire to illuminate paths forward, it's being weaponized by first degree witch-hunt and wielded as a torch of anger and division. Movements that should inspire unity now breed resentment. We see men ostracized from roles not because they're unqualified but because they're men. Equality is now achieved by the obliteration of men. True progress in their eyes lies now in perpetuating division and not fostering partnerships. There is nothing wrong with advocating for women's access to essential healthcare, such as contraception and abortion services, in the face of incest or sexual game without consent are undeniably important. These measures are legal and critical in ensuring that women have control over their bodies and can pursue social and economic mobility without unnecessary restrictions.

One evening, I settled into the comfort of my living room after work. The soft glow of dim lighting stretching long shadows across the walls. On the west side, a peacock painting commanded attention, its vibrant colors standing out against the more muted tones of the room. Beneath it, a palm tree in a decorative flower pot added a touch of nature, its fronds gently swaying in the cool, air-conditioned breeze. Above the TV, a series of butterfly mirrors, delicately arranged in shimmering patterns, adorned the wall. Their golden frames reflected the soft light, creating a subtle play of radiance.

The clock, with its ticking echoes, marked the passing time in the background. All of this surrounded me as I sat on my sofa, a bottle of water resting beside me, the seat buried under a small mountain of books. As I settled into my couch, flipping through the pages of *When the Clock Broke: Con Men, Conspiracists, and How America Cracked Up in the Early 1990s* by John Ganz, my thoughts drifted through the intricate world of political upheaval and social chaos of the past. My attention would be pulled towards the screen. Kamala Harris, the Vice President of the United States, appeared before the nation, her voice bold and unmistakable. I set the book down, leaning forward as her words filled the room.

Ideally, she wasn't the kind of figure I'd normally stop everything to watch. I had other preferences. She is around the same age as my mother just that my mom is forever young. Despite her position in the American political sphere, was not the ideal subject of my attention only in that moment, the significance of the conversation became undeniable. This was no trivial matter—it was a pivotal point in history, one where words spoken by those in power had real consequences. I had read her book, familiarized myself with how her name was properly pronounced, and reflected on her days in California.

I understood the layers of her history—the experiences that shaped her rise to the vice presidency. But even with all of that context, it became clear that her role in this moment, and the one that she was contesting for as important as it was, would always exist in the shadow of the past. Her tenure as vice president, for all its challenges and achievements, I believe would forever be measured against the earlier chapters of her career, and the history that came before her.

The statements that day—accusing men she disagreed with on policy and reform as perpetuators of violence, comparing President Donald Trump to Chancellor Adolf Hitler of Germany, the leader who is immortalized as a taboo that it's practically illegal or forbidden to reference his name alongside, laws mobilized to block the promotion of his Nazi ideology, including the display of his image due to the atrocities committed under his regime peculiarly nearing his occupancy period—felt like jarring notes in a symphony that was already struggling to stay in tune.

The ice of her words seemed to shift the atmosphere around me. Here I was, surrounded by objects that represented both peace and life —nature, beauty, and the written word—and yet I found myself caught in the storm of political discourse. Her remarks, while designed to provoke, felt like a stark reminder of the polarization and hyperbole that had taken over public discourse. I watched, my curiosity growing as her rhetoric painted men with a broad, destructive brush, my mind racing to process the implications.

How, I wondered, could such rhetoric, so divisive and exaggerated, help us navigate the real challenges at hand? There, in that moment, with the soft murmur of my TV and the clutter of books around me, I realized how far we had come from the ideals of reasoned debate, Geneva conventions and balanced leadership. The more she spoke, the more I found myself questioning not just the substance of her claims, but the broader trajectory of our global political landscape.

I am neither a political commentator nor a host

for any Late-Night Show. And I certainly don't need to be an American before I take a stance or climb to the top of the Empire State Building. What I do know is that such inflammatory remarks, though designed to stir emotions, fall short when evaluated against the principles of leadership that resonate with any democratic electorate. Elections, at their crust, are about competence and vision. Voters seek someone who can address their everyday concerns with practical solutions and wisdom, not someone who resorts to history's darkest moments to win arguments.

I have experienced these metrics before, whether I was the one vying for votes or campaigning for others, or merely on the sidelines, from the supervised environment of creche to the coded ranches of college, during student elections.

I was groomed that the true measure of a leader materializes in their ability to uplift, unite, and inspire, not to create false dichotomies that detract from the real issues of governance. Gender equality today seems less about celebrating the value of all individuals and breaking down the barriers that hold them back, and more about attacking one group. The focus has shifted from creating opportunities for everyone to a divisive approach that undermines true progress.

Let me take a detour from the usual lanes

of debate and steer us into a topic you might not have given much thought to: cars. Now, I'm not exactly the person you'd turn to for advice on engine maintenance or tips on trading in your sedan for something flashier. In fact, my automotive expertise pretty much ends at knowing which pedal makes the car go. I'm the kind of person who thinks "horsepower" refers to how fast I can Google "why is my car making that sound?" But, like many of you, I know a few folks who are passionate about cars. They can wax poetic about great vehicles the way foodies rave about a perfect crème brûlée. But there's something fascinating—and occasionally infuriating—about the current conversation around cars, especially when it intersects with broader debates about climate change, innovation, and the future of transportation.

The push to abandon petrol and diesel vehicles—or worse, to give up cars altogether—has gone beyond a national issue; it's now a global traffic jam. Don't get me wrong: I admire Elon Musk, the rocket guy, that North Korea's defense budget can't compete with his memes probably more than President Trump or any of his kids do. The man gave us electric cars, *optimist* and a flamethrower, which is great idea, and undeniably cool. But here's the thing: electric cars aren't only *the* future—they're just *part* of the future. They're like kale in a salad: useful, but not the whole meal. Sure, they reduce tailpipe emissions, but what about the environmental toll of mining for lithium or the fact that charging stations don't grow on trees?

And let's not forget that many parts of the world still power their electric grids with coal, making the "green" car argument look a little gray. The relentless vilification of petrol and oil is reaching absurd levels, and it's enough to drive even the calmest among us up the wall. Let's pause and look at the facts: oil is not some malevolent force scheming in dark corners to destroy the planet. It's a resource—a powerful one, no doubt—like water, sunlight, or wind. The real issue isn't its existence; it's our choices in how we use and manage it. But try making that distinction in today's charged climate debate, where nuance is often drowned out by slogans and outrage.

Take Greta Thunberg, for example. There's no denying her ability to inspire millions or her impressive commitment to the cause. Her fiery speeches have become the rallying cry for climate action, and for that, she deserves credit. But passion without precision can only take the conversation so far. More often than not, her critiques zero in on corporations, casting them as pantomime villains while glossing over the complex realities of energy systems and the practical challenges of transitioning to a low-carbon economy.

The reality is that oil isn't the sole enemy of our

environment. It's a resource that has powered economies, connected continents, and lifted millions out of poverty. It's not a question of "use it or lose it" but rather a question of balance: how do we harness it responsibly while investing in cleaner alternatives? This isn't a zero-sum game, but the narrative often treats it as such, lumping oil into a simplistic "good versus evil" framework. Corporations such as: Ford, GM, and the rest of the big players. Are they blameless? Certainly not. But neither are they the sole culprits in this story. They're caught in a strange position—like teenagers being yelled at by both their parents and their friends. Governments and activists are demanding that they go electric yesterday.

The very people they are supposed to be creating better policies for, millions of them drivers, are saying, "Sure, we'll go electric... just as soon as you make it affordable, convenient, and not require a full PhD to understand how to charge it".

Corporations like the Volkswagen Group, Renault Group, and Bentley have built incredible reputations through decades of innovation, offering everything from compact sedans to luxury SUVs, high-performance sports cars, and cutting-edge electric vehicles. Their engineering feats include the renowned Quattro all-wheel-drive system, advanced infotainment technology, and top-tier safety features that have set new standards in the automotive industry. These companies don't just make cars —they create driving experiences that blend performance, technology, and luxury.

These federations pouring billions into renewable energy and greener technologies not out of sheer altruism, but because they recognize the shifting tides blowing from the Middle East to the exhaust pipes and turbines of the mainstream world. It's progress that deserves recognition, not dismissal. As more employers switch to electric vehicles, embrace liberal ideologies, and promote vegetarianism, there's an underlying assumption that everyone, regardless of age or ability, can easily adapt to these changes. But this one-size-fits-all mentality ignores the reality that not everyone is equipped to keep up with the rapid shift. For many seniors of my father's generation, the world of smartphones, email, and instant messaging feels foreign and, frankly, overwhelming.

They were raised in a time when paper letters and face-to-face interactions were the norm— simple, tangible forms of communication that didn't require tech know-how. Today's push to go paperless in nearly every facet of life— from healthcare and government notifications to business communications—leaves many dropping behind and penalized. This isn't just about convenience, preference, or vegetable picking. For those without the skills or access to navigate the digital world, these changes represent a profound barrier.

And it's not just the elderly; many people of all ages, particularly in rural or underserved communities, or recent migrants are at a distinct disadvantage as technology advances at breakneck speed. We've come to expect that everyone is a digital native and has a cousin who works in Silicon Valley, Skolkovo or East London Tech City but we're transgressing that entire generations of people were never granted the tools or training to thrive in a tech-centric society.

The totalitarianism here is in the assumption that everyone can and should conform to a new way of living and communicating without considering the material, practical limitations many face. Yes, the future is proverbially, predictably and provenly electric, and yes, we should strive to be more sustainable. But as we push forward, we cannot forget that these changes will take time—and we can't expect the next generation to carry the trammel of the transition without support or preparation colonoscopy. Imagine growing up in the 1950s or 1960s, when patrol cars were a common sight and paper was the primary mode of communication.

For someone from that era, adjusting to today's tech-driven world must feel like being cast adrift.

It was because they were away or unserious during the technological advancement era, they were focused on shaping the world and providing for their families, furnished the inventors the stability and peace of mind they needed to think, create, and innovate. When affliction strikes, it's not just a battle with health —it's a struggle to stay connected to a society that has rapidly evolved beyond what they know. These individuals, who grew up with face-to-face conversations and handwritten letters, are now thrust into a digital world that demands they understand apps, websites, and new technology in order to survive.

This takes me back to a recent dialogue I had with a British conscientious man approaching the 80 lodestar; frail but dignified, carries the prestige of his years with a quiet grace and gripped sophistication. His silver hair, once thick and dark, is now thin and wispy, framing a face marked by time—a tapestry of wrinkles, each one telling a bestiary of a life well-lived from his struggling childhood to his days as a cook in a restaurant to his heroic service in a cabinet role in the affairs of Scotland. His eyes, though clouded with age, still hold a sharpness, a flicker of the wit and wisdom that comes from decades of experience. His voice rich in the hefty Scottish accent, gravelly tenor, softened but unmistakably commanding.

He drives with a quiet elegance just like myself, no rushing, no hesitation—just smooth, controlled movements. His memory sharper when it comes to roads, directions, and landmarks, and he drives with the confidence that comes from knowing exactly where he's headed. He had just recovered from a serious presbycusis and he shared that, in some ways, he wished he hadn't survived. It wasn't just the physical pain he struggled with—it was the overwhelming feeling of being left behind in a world that no longer feels familiar.

A world that expects him to keep up, despite the fact that everything he once knew is now obsolete and he is categorized as just a statistic in a "moronic" digital transformation, irrespective of his authenticity, decimal points in his bank accounts or just ordinary basic necessities for survival and reconciliation.

CHAPTER NINE:

THE GIANT
MIDDLE FINGER
OF DEMOCRACY

"When the righteous are in authority,
the people rejoice;
but when the wicked rule,
the people groan."
Proverbs 29:2

I n Africa, a room is more than four walls, a roof, and a sanctuary for the human occupant. It is an ecosystem, a shared existence, where the idea of possession is quietly challenged by the indomitable will of nature's smallest creatures. You may pay the rent, you may choose the curtains, and you may fumigate with zealous determination. But in the end, your room is not yours alone.

Among the silent cohabitants are the spiders, those mysterious artisans of the class *Araneidae*. Their webs are both architectural wonders and existential traps, a blend of beauty and brutality. These creatures, with their deliberate or darting movements, seem like sentinels of an unseen realm. Their eight unblinking eyes hold a quiet wisdom—or perhaps an indifference—that makes one ponder humanity's preoccupation with control. Yet, they are but guests in this hierarchy of life.

The true rulers of this hidden kingdom are the cockroaches—nature's unsung champions of resilience and survival. If democracy had an avatar, it would wear the antennae of a cockroach, and double up as an ambassador for the insecta civilization. These emissaries of the class *Blattodea* hold no regard for boundaries, hierarchies, or even the sanctity of human discomfort. They do not discriminate in their invasions; they embody an egalitarianism that philosophers might envy.

Bold and unapologetic, they loiter in bathrooms, patrol corridors like prison guards, and occasionally engage in what can only be described as a comedic dance of pursuit. When the day retires and the room dims, they emerge from the cracks and crevices—the tiniest fractures in our imagined dominion—to reclaim what they perceive as theirs.

No corner is too sacred, no secret hole too small. Cockroaches thrive not because they conquer but because they adapt quickly. They find opportunity in adversity, persistence in the face of opposition. Humanity, so often caught in the illusion of dominion, could learn something from their silent diplomacy. They share space without permission, but they do so with a remarkable balance—never destroying the person, merely existing.

There are moments in life when reality outpaces fiction, and one of those moments happened in the dead of night, in a room ruled not just by its human occupants but by the silent, scuttling empire of cockroaches. It all began when one particularly audacious cockroach decided that my brother Bright's left ear was a portal worth exploring. Yes, his *ear*.

What followed was a scene straight out of

a survival thriller—equal parts horrifying and resourceful, with a touch of unintended Trevor Noah comedy. Bright's plight wasn't just a test of his patience but a family challenge. In a world without the conveniences of 24-hour ambulance services or late-night hospitals (this wasn't Great Britain, where ambulances roar at all hours), you had to improvise. And that's exactly what our dad did. With no doctors available until at least half past nine the next morning—and definitely not on a Friday night, because weekends, apparently, are sacred for practitioners—Dad took matters into his own hands.

Armed with nothing more than boiled water, a syringe, and sheer determination, he executed what can only be described as the first unofficial insect removal procedure. Meticulously, without any medical training, he filled the syringe with water that was hot but not scalding and, with a precision that would make any field medic proud, pushed the water into Bright's ear. Out came the water, and with it, the rogue cockroach, presumably more traumatized than anyone involved.

Now, let me be clear: this is not a recommendation for at-home medical procedures. Don't try this even if you're in a similarly desperate situation with no medical assistance in sight. Call your GP. But desperate times called for desperate measures, and to Dad's credit, it miraculously worked. By the hour, Bright's ear was back to normal, perhaps even sharper than before—though I suspect the clarity may have been more psychological than auditory.

In the aftermath of this midnight ordeal, Bright declared an all-out war on our insect overlords. With boiling water as our weapon of choice, he and I launched a campaign against the cockroaches, blissfully unaware of the futility of our mission. After all, these creatures are not just resilient; they are among the planet's oldest and most populous organisms.

Two kids blazed with not kettles but boiled water stored in a sealed bottle with a precision-drilled hole at the top stood little chance against evolution's finest survivors, especially without corporate sponsorship from; Unilever. But we didn't care, because in our childhood zeal it inspired midnight heroics. This isn't a chapter about the demographics or the infestations of cockroaches, or their unwelcome appearances in our kitchens and corridors or even that faithful misfortune.

This is about their surprising aptitude for democratic decision-making. Unlike the organized colonies of bees or ants, with their hierarchical queens and industrious workers, cockroaches live without elaborate social structures. But manage to make collective decisions with remarkable efficiency. One evening, as kids, my brother Bright, two other friends, and I unwittingly stumbled upon an outstanding phenomenon that dawn as two equal parts of innocent curiosity and accidental brilliance. We had left three empty boxes shaped like shelters in a corner of the house. They were discarded boxes that housed crate of eggs that mom brought from the market earlier. To the casual observer, it might have looked like mere clutter. But by morning, the scene had transformed into what seemed like an impromptu experiment straight out of a behavioral science textbook. As we approached, we noticed the telltale scurrying of cockroaches —more than 20 of them, ranging from the robustly sizable to the more modestly scaled.

These uninvited tenants had wasted no time making themselves at home, each box now a potential sanctuary. But what struck us wasn't just their eagerness to seek refuge; it was their orderliness. Rather than piling chaotically into a single space or competing in a Darwinian battle for dominance, they had divided themselves with mathematical precision. Two groups of 10 occupied two shelters, leaving the third box conspicuously empty. It was as though they instinctively grasped the limits of space and resources, creating a balance without the need for leaders, speeches, or conflict. This display of collective organization wasn't just impressive; it was thought-provoking and beyond vintage.

How, without any apparent

communication, could these creatures—so often dismissed as pests—demonstrate such an innate understanding of balance and coexistence? What appeared to be a simple gathering of cockroaches was, in fact, a masterclass in resource management. They had a revolutionary consensus. Years later, in high school, I would discover the fascinating science behind this childhood observation as well as in the class of Dr. Kingsley Badu of KNUST. Cockroaches, members of the phylum Arthropoda, are remarkable creatures with segmented bodies, jointed appendages, and a knack for evolutionary survival.

However, it isn't just their physical design that sets them apart—it's their ability to balance cooperation and competition so elegantly. Without the need for bureaucratic committees, economic debates, or even a shared language, cockroaches embody a pragmatic form of democracy. They avoid overcrowding, hoarding, or succumbing to endless chaos. Instead, they assess their surroundings with uncanny precision, seamlessly adapting their group dynamics to the resources available.

The sixteenth President of the United States, Abraham Lincoln's immortal words, "government of the people, by the people, for the people," have long been the golden standard for democratic ideals. In my over two decades on the planet, I have observed the state of democracies worldwide, I can't help but feel we've turned those words into a fairytale—a comforting myth we tell ourselves while the reality veers far from the script. Across continents, from Afghanistan to Africa to America, democracy too often seems like an elaborate stage production: grand in design, hollow in delivery.

In the country dubbed as the roundabout of the ancient world and also a bedrock to Farhad Darya, a celebrated Afghan singer, songwriter, and composer. He is widely regarded as one of the most influential and beloved artists of the world and often referred to as "Voice of Afghanistan" for his role in uniting diverse ethnic groups through music and promoting peace, cultural pride, and social change; a nation that became the poster child for democracy's potential in the post-9/11 era.

For two decades, global powers poured in resources, rhetoric, and military might to transform a war-torn land into a bastion of democracy. Elections were held, new leaders were paraded as reformers, and the promise of progress dangled like a beacon of hope over a population battered by decades of conflict. But as history has shown, the foundation beneath this façade was far from solid. The democratic project in Afghanistan was never as empowering as it seemed. On legislation documents, elections gave Afghans the right to choose their leaders, however, the reality was that true power resided elsewhere.

Warlords who controlled regions with militias and terror, foreign powers pursuing their own strategic interests, and an ever-lurking Taliban resistant to democratic ideals were the real arbiters of Afghan destiny.

The ballot box may have symbolized a shimmering hope, but in practice, it was overshadowed by guns, intimidation, and the ever-present specter of corruption. When the U.S. withdrawal began in earnest in 2021, the fragility of this democratic experiment was laid bare. Districts fell one after another in a domino effect, not to grassroots uprisings, but to calculated ambushes and tactical takeovers by the Taliban. Provincial capitals that were supposed to be bastions of the Afghan government's authority became scenes of chaos and capitulation. Soldiers, often unpaid and unsupported, surrendered or fled.

Officials who once spoke of resilience quietly negotiated their exits or switched allegiances. The swiftness of the Taliban's advance was chilling. With a strategy blending brute force and psychological warfare, they seized towns and cities almost unopposed. In some cases, they ambushed military convoys and slaughtered soldiers who had no choice but to surrender. In others, they staged massacres in villages to send a brutal message: resistance was futile. Perhaps the most heart-wrenching was the fall of Kabul. In the early days of the withdrawal, officials reassured the world that the capital was secure, that democracy would endure even in the face of adversity. But those reassurances proved close to nothing.

The Taliban swept into the city with barely a shot fired, and the world watched in disbelief as Afghan citizens clung desperately to departing planes at the airport—some falling to their deaths in their bid for escape. For the Afghan people, this wasn't just a political collapse; it was an existential betrayal. The democracy they had been promised—built with blood, sweat, and immeasurable suffering—was revealed as a mirage. Their voices, their votes, their aspirations, were all rendered meaningless in the face of power dynamics they could not control. The international community, so vocal about Afghanistan's democratic future, now seemed stunned into silence. Foreign leaders who had championed intervention as a moral obligation suddenly retreated, offering platitudes about lessons learned while the Afghan people were left to grapple with the ruins.

The aftermath of the Taliban's return was brutal. Reports of retributive killings surfaced. Women, who had made strides in education and employment under the democratic regime, were forced back into the shadows of oppression. The promises of inclusion and liberty made to an entire generation were shattered overnight. Afghanistan's tragedy is not just a story of failed policy or poor execution—it is a stark indictment of what happens when democracy is imposed as a veneer rather than cultivated from within. Decisions affecting the lives of millions of Afghans were made not in Kabul but in Washington, Brussels, and other distant capitals. Their aspirations were subverted by global geopolitics and the entrenched power of local warlords.

This collapse wasn't inevitable; it was the product of decades of missteps. From the exclusion of key stakeholders in the early days of nation-building to the short-sightedness of propping up a government riddled with corruption, every step paved the way for the tragedy that unfolded in 2021. Democracy had been dropped in by parachute and enforced by military occupation. It was not allowed to grow organically, rooted in the culture, traditions, and aspirations of the people it seeks to serve. I met her at Waterstones on Sauchiehall Street in Glasgow, a chance encounter among the shelves. She was browsing titles, the image of calm in a place built for introspection. But as I struck up a conversation, her story unfolded— a story that was anything but tranquil. She had fled Afghanistan with her family, their escape a whirlwind spanning two harrowing weeks.

First, they crossed into Pakistan, then found refuge in the Netherlands, and finally made it to the UK. It was a journey that defied reason, filled with fear, desperation, and a glimmer of hope that somehow refused to extinguish. She told me her story in English—a language her parents had taught her in secret, under the cover of darkness, in a land where education for girls was often an act of defiance. She had never been allowed to attend school. Speaking English within her homeland was dangerous, a risk her parents took because they believed, against all odds, in the power of knowledge. Her voice trembled not with agony, but with the vividness of memory.

The collapse of Afghanistan in 2021 was more than a political failure—it was a betrayal. I saw the images on the cable news just like everyone one else. The promises of democracy, long touted by foreign powers, had always been tenuous at best, and the speed with which the nation fell back into chaos was a bitter confirmation. Warlords, corruption, and foreign interests had always held the reins, and the ballots in the hands of everyday Afghans had been little more than symbolic paperweights. She was thankful to the bravery of her family's escape, like so many others, which was born of necessity.

The Taliban's resurgence meant that those who could flee, did so. Those who couldn't? They were left behind to navigate a grim reality where decisions were no longer made in the halls of government or the polling stations but at the barrel of a gun, or in the UK a knock at the door for a post or unintended social media hypothetical comment. This is the world we inhabit—a world where democracy is too often reduced to a slogan.

From Harare to Kampala or Maputo to Kigali, democracies exist in name only, manipulated by leaders who have mastered the art of using democratic structures to entrench their power. The result has been a disillusioned populace. Professor P.L.O Lumumba with his critical assets: a big brain of nkrumahism, a spine of steel and axe to grind cannot defy the black rock and sheer light on the ubuntu spirit alone. Robert Mugabe's nearly four-decade rule, elections were held regularly. But they were hardly democratic. Voters faced coercion and intimidation, opposition parties were muzzled, and the media was tightly controlled.

The country operated under a system designed to maintain the illusion of democracy while keeping power concentrated in the hands of Mugabe and his inner circle. The people went to the polls, but the outcome was never truly in their hands. It was governance built on treachery and manipulation, cloaked in the language of democracy. President Yoweri Museveni has clung to power since 1986, winning election after election in a political landscape shaped by intimidation and violence. Opposition figures, such as Bobi Wine, have faced brutal crackdowns, with supporters beaten and arrested, and campaign activities disrupted. In Uganda, the façade of democracy is meticulously maintained, but the substance—free and fair elections, respect for dissent, and accountability —remains elusive. The people may cast their votes, but the system is rigged to ensure that Museveni's grip on power remains unshaken.

Mozambique, meanwhile, offers a tragic juxtaposition of political dysfunction and resource potential. The nation, rich in natural gas reserves, has been mired in cycles of violence and corruption. Elections are plagued by allegations of fraud, and political power remains concentrated among elites who benefit from deals with foreign companies. The promises of democratic governance have done little to alleviate widespread poverty or stem the violence in the northern regions, where insurgencies have displaced hundreds of thousands.

For many Mozambicans, democracy is an abstraction, disconnected from the daily struggle for survival. Rwanda, under Paul Kagame, tells yet another complex story. Kagame's leadership has been lauded for transforming Kigali into a pillar of progress and modernity, with clean streets, economic growth, and technological innovation. Yet this progress comes at the cost of political freedoms. Elections in Rwanda are foregone conclusions, with Kagame routinely winning with suspiciously high margins. Opposition voices are stifled, and dissent is met with swift, often brutal, retaliation. It's a stark example of a "developmental autocracy," where economic gains are prioritized over democratic rights, leaving the world to grapple with the question: can progress and freedom coexist?

Ghana often celebrated as a beacon of democracy in Africa, has a story with two sides of a coin that is both inspiring and deeply troubling. In a region marked by political instability and authoritarian regimes, Ghana has achieved what many other nations aspire to: peaceful elections, stable transfers of power, and a relatively free press. Its civil society is vibrant, and its democratic institutions, at least on the surface, appear robust. Yet, beneath this ice of stability lies a more sobering reality—one that raises questions about the true cost of its democratic experiment.

Corruption remains a persistent blight on Ghana's governance. Public funds, meant to address pressing issues like education, healthcare, and infrastructure, are too often siphoned off by those entrusted to lead. Scandals involving misappropriated resources erode public trust and reinforce the perception that democracy, for all its ideals, has not delivered for the average Ghanaian. Economic inequality remains rife, with wealth concentrated among the elite, while rural and marginalized communities struggle to access basic services. For many, the democratic promise of equality and opportunity seems more like a distant dream than a lived reality.

Imagine the elation of a young scholar, their hard work rewarded with an opportunity to further their education on the world stage. They board their flights with dreams of academic excellence and a determination to bring their knowledge back home to contribute to national development. But upon arrival in a foreign country, their aspirations are met not with the support they were promised, but with silence—a deafening reminder of the betrayal they have yet to comprehend. The promised government funding, the lifeline that would sustain them through their studies, never materializes. Stranded in a land far from home, they are left to navigate an unfamiliar system without resources or support. Some resort to working menial jobs, sacrificing their studies just to afford basic necessities. Others face the gut-wrenching decision of abandoning their education altogether, their dreams reduced to survival in a foreign land. These are not isolated incidents but recurring tragedies, emblematic of a broader failure of leadership.

Scholarship programs that should empower

the next generation of leaders instead become balloon gestures, announced with pomp and ceremony but devoid of follow-through. The message is clear: talent and ambition, no matter how extraordinary, are expendable in a system that prioritizes appearances over accountability. This foolishness is more than a financial lapse; it's a moral one. These young scholars represent Ghana's best and brightest, the very individuals who could drive innovation, policy reform, and economic development. Instead, they are left abandoned, their potential wasted, their faith in their country eroded. For a nation that prides itself on its democratic ideals and commitment to progress, this systemic failure is a damning indictment. Ghana's future is being squandered, not by lack of talent or opportunity, but by the greed and negligence of those entrusted to lead.

I know this because I have walked this unforeseeable thorny path of unforgiving deception. I bear the scars of this treachery —silent wounds etched beneath the sheath of resilience and substitutionary grace.

The self-proclaimed beacon of democracy, with stars and stripes in their national flag, the cracks in its foundation are growing harder to ignore. The ideal of every citizen having an equal voice—a hallmark of democracy— is often overshadowed by the grim reality of money-fueled politics and a two-party system that prioritizes power over the public good.

In this system, campaigns become less about ideas and more about who can raise the most money to saturate airwaves with attack ads and flashy soundbites. Corporate interests pour billions into elections, drowning out the voices of everyday citizens and leaving the democratic process feeling more like a rigged casino than a celebration of civic participation.

Nowhere has this erosion of democratic ideals been more evident than in the internal coup within the Democratic Party of America during the last presidential cycle. As whispers of doubt about President Joe Biden's age and vigor began to dominate headlines, party insiders moved decisively to edge him out of the spotlight. Kamala Harris, once the vice president and a polarizing figure in her own right, was positioned as the preferred candidate. But what was framed as a pragmatic adjustment quickly revealed itself as an insidious power play, one that ignored the will of many Democratic voters. The maneuver backfired spectacularly, alienating key constituencies and contributing to a stunning loss that should be an admonition hubris masquerading as strategy.

Voter suppression laws acted from the peaches of Georgia to the progressive kingdom of Mali make it harder for marginalized communities to participate in elections. Gerrymandering persists in skewing representation, allowing politicians to select their voters instead of voters choosing their representatives. The rise of J.D. Vance stands as a peculiar testament to a democracy shaped by the leadership of insistent miracles of clear-headed values rather than the self-serving spectacle and shallow theatrics that dominate today's political landscape, where substance and common sense often take a backseat. The advent of online voting, projected to be a modern solution, has also opened the door for potential fraud and manipulation, further eroding public trust in a system that was once seen as progressively strong and unshakable.

Estonia's digital infrastructure has garnered global admiration. This emerges with the uncomfortable realization that, in a country so reliant on technology, any blip who regulates this landscape wields enormous power over their democratic process. Power to the people has become the biggest cliche of my lifetime, whether in emerging nations in Africa or the grownups in the West.

For all my life, I had been bloodbath and sold the stories that authoritarian regimes, especially those of China and Singapore, were on a path to inevitable decline—oppressive, stifling, and were ultimately doomed. The more I reflect on the current global landscape, the more I am struck by how out of sync this narrative is with reality. Republic of China is painted as a cold and monolithic authoritarian power. However, continues to thrive economically and technologically, and the younger generation of Chinese citizens seems more eager than ever to return home after studying abroad, most of these are long-term friends I have made. If China's political system was as suffocating and straining as we have been led to believe, why then are so many of its brightest minds not only committed to returning but also eager to contribute to their country's ongoing transformation?

Singapore on the other end is dismissed as a mere puppet state controlled by a ruling elite. Despite the absence of the Western democratic ideal, Singapore stands as one of the most prosperous and efficient nations in the world. With a thriving economy, robust infrastructure, and a high standard of living, it is clear that Singapore's brand of governance, may not portray the atomization of a Western democratic standards, but has delivered surgical stability and growth in ways many democracies struggle to achieve. The country's pragmatic approach to governance—emphasizing competence, order, and progress over ideological purity—has allowed it to become a global hub of commerce, innovation, and social harmony. What has become increasingly apparent is the frequency of distinction between the political dysfunction that plagues many Western democracies and the unmatched universal stability displayed across China and Singapore.

Today, the tidal waves have shifted focus and there are countless number of people from all around the globe including the West who are seeking opportunities in these very labelled "authoritarian" states. Friends and colleagues who became disillusioned with the political and economic climate in their home countries have relocated to China, not as refugees fleeing oppression, but as individuals seeking a better quality of life. In China, the cost of living is lower, infrastructure is cutting-edge, and social services are reliable. The allure of China's economic dynamism and the practical benefits of living there are undeniable. Singapore's model of governance, with its emphasis on order, long-term planning, and minimal corruption, has proven far more efficient than the fractured, gridlocked politics of many Western nations.

Watch this: right now, as I capitalize and progress on conjuring and canceling of thoughts to be put here, its past midnight, and I am precisely typing this chapter on my MacBook. I am wrapped in a hoodie and track pants and lying beside the heater in my living room. I cannot help but notice how my thoughts are interrupted, not by profound revelations or the whistles of the passing cars or the kids upstairs jumping and playing in their beds, but by the constant breeze of warmth of the heater trying—and failing—to stave off the chill of a -1°C winter night.

The heater, which offers an enduring moment of warmth, only exacerbates my growing anxiety as it rakes up an energy bill that, in the long run, will far outstrip the temporary comfort it provides. And as I wrestle with the cold and the mounting costs, I find myself, somewhat reluctantly, pondering the state of the systems that govern us. I'm not claiming that authoritarianism is inherently superior to democracy, but I can't help but reflect on the present reality with growing unease. In this Western home, equipped with modern technology, the very comforts that should mean a functioning society seem increasingly unsustainable.

Political gridlock, escalating inflation, and rising utility bills are far from the promises of democratic governance—freedom, equality, accountability—all of which seem more like distant ideals than practical realities. In moments like this, when personal survival is threatened by the cold and the cost of staying warm, it's hard not to consider the apparent efficiency of authoritarian systems.

Those systems, for all their flaws, are able to prioritize stability, long-term planning, and decision-making in ways that seem elusive in today's fractured democracies. Back in Africa, the people I know—friends, family, acquaintances—look at my life in the West and see only what they want to see: prosperity, privilege, success. Their imaginations paint my existence in hues of luxury and abundance, untainted by the daily grind of survival. "When will you send me the latest iPhone?" they ask, the words lighthearted but heavy with expectation, as if such extravagance is simply a byproduct of living in the so-called First World.

The irony is sharp and unrelenting. Here I am, juggling bills, cutting corners, and bracing myself for the next financial shock, while those far away see me as a benefactor of endless fortune. The dissonance between perception and reality is staggering. They see the polished surface of a Western existence—the gadgets, the photos, the anecdotes of opportunity—and mistake it for ease. What they don't see are the mounting stresses of a faltering system: the escalating cost of energy that keeps the heater running through a biting winter night, the relentless inflation that erodes purchasing power, or the creeping anxiety that shadows every financial decision.

They don't understand that even in the wealthiest nations, the machinery of governance can falter, leaving many of us to fend for ourselves amid the promises of democracy that increasingly ring voidness. This disconnect doesn't just frustrate—it exposes the profound absurdity of it all. They ask for luxury items as though they are a given, while I wrestle with the growing realization that the systems I've come to depend on are crumbling. It's a sobering truth that forces me to confront an uncomfortable question: if democracy, in its loftiest ideals, was meant to secure equality and opportunity, why does it feel so unprepared to address the very real struggles of those living within it? Is it any wonder that, in such moments, I begin to wonder if the much-maligned authoritarian regime systems might be better equipped—however imperfectly—to navigate crises, manage resources, and prioritize collective well-being?

This isn't an endorsement of communism, authoritarianism, fascism or President Xi Jinping and his signature policies; including the *Belt and Road Initiative* and *Made in China 2025* or the militarization of the South China Sea. Whether he is viewed as a visionary or a despot, undoubtedly has left an indelible mark on both China and the world. This is also definitely not about Prime Minister Lee Hsien Loong, who after graduating from Harvard University's Kennedy School of Government returned home to foster the legacy of his father. This is a great testament of the acknowledgment of the undeniable failures in practice, cracks in the democratic façade which has become harder to ignore.

Federal government and elected officials always have their motorcades tearing through traffic in small towns and big cities with an urgency that demands attention and a parallel parking of other commuters—siren laden and flashes of lights to showcase their self-importance and authority, meanwhile this apparent haste vanishes within the corridors of officialdom, where inefficiency, indecision, and lethargy reign supreme in our current world.

CHAPTER TEN:

COMMONSENSE RELINQUISHED FOR SENSITIVITY

"For the time is coming
when people will not endure
sound teaching,
but having itching ears
they will accumulate for
themselves teachers to
suit their own likings."
2 Timothy 3: 4

F or much of human history, education has been the cornerstone of human progress —the crucible in which civilization itself was forged. It was not merely a path to self-betterment but the very essence of societal transformation, a force that reshaped empires, redefined cultures, and propelled humanity toward uncharted frontiers. From the hallowed halls of ancient academies in Athens, where philosophy and democracy were birthed, to the technological innovation hubs of Silicon Valley, education has served as the relentless engine of invention, discovery, and enlightenment.

Through the harnessing of fire, the cultivation of crops, the discovery of electricity, the splitting of the atom and the unraveling of the mysteries of physics that sent humanity beyond the bounds of Earth, education has proven itself indispensable. The toothpaste that freshens our mornings, the vaccines that obliterate diseases, and the semiconductors that power the digital age are all branches of a tree rooted in centuries of learning and inquiry. Education was not just a tool; it was revered as a deity—a god whose worship promised understanding, salvation, and mastery over the chaos of the unknown.

From Braeside to Brisbane or from

Yokohama to Yamoussoukro, Education bore an almost sacred covenant, a luminous beacon for those desperate to escape the relentless cycles of poverty and despair. It wasn't merely a stepping stone; it was a messiah, a protocol of hope passed down from one generation to the next. For countless families, education represented far more than the acquisition of knowledge—it was the embodiment of progress, a tangible promise of a better tomorrow. In its pursuit, sacrifices were boundless.

African parents sold their livestock, dismantled their heirlooms, and forfeited their own comforts, often going without so their children could sit in a classroom, don a uniform, and wield the humble but powerful tool of a pencil. Schools were sanctuaries, hallowed grounds where dreams were nurtured and potential unfolded. The walls of these institutions carried the whispers of countless aspirations, while teachers stood as revered figures—guardians of ambition and custodians of hope. They were not merely instructors but stewards of a collective future, entrusted with the sacred duty of transforming lives and shaping destinies.

This institution woven itself into the very fabric of existence, its value transcending individual ambition to promise something far greater: collective upliftment. It was the ladder of possibility, rising from the dusty fields of farmers, the humble workshops of laborers, and the improbable stalls of traders, offering their children a path to transcend their circumstances. To those who dared to climb, it held the promise of stepping into new worlds as doctors, engineers, scholars, leaders, singers, and a transcendent.

This reverence for education was not just palpable; it was elemental. Its pursuit mirrored the pursuit of freedom itself—a yearning to transcend the limitations of the present and grasp the infinite potential of the future. Education was not just seen as a privilege but as the cornerstone of human dignity, the mechanism through which the most profound human desires—for meaning, purpose, and progress—could be realized.

From the eloquence of Barack Obama to the clinical precision of Ben Carson or from the intellectual provocations of Jordan Peterson to the unyielding wit of Piers Morgan, education stands as the silent architect of their stature. It is the great enabler, the engine behind their influence, and the foundation of their legacy. Rich or poor, revered or reviled, their stories are etched into history because of the transformative power of learning. Education, in its purest form, is the great alchemist—turning potential into greatness, giving voice to the unheard, and refining thought into action. It was education that lifted humanity from caves to cathedrals, from simple survival to the sophistication of civilizations.

It gave us the ability to cure diseases that once ravaged entire populations, to unlock the mysteries of the atom, and to refine the very food we eat. It is education that has seeded hope in barren wombs, engineered the codes that govern machines, and elevated common sense into profound reasoning. It is, perhaps, the closest humanity has come to wielding divine power—a force so transformative it feels sacred. I was informed, I held tight to the mantra: *Go to school, study hard, and you can be whoever you want to be.* These weren't just words; they were a creed, passed down like a holy relic. It wasn't a cliché to me; it was a divine commandment, as absolute as gravity and just as enabling.

To believe in it was to believe in the limitless possibilities of effort, discipline, and determination. It was a promise whispered into the ears of dreamers and a call to action for those daring to break free from the chains of circumstance. I worshipped that belief. It gave me more than hope—it gave me agency. It framed my world, gave me purpose, and demanded my reverence. Educational proclivities became a sanctified path, the only one worth treading. It granted me friends and adversaries, opened doors to knowledge, and set before me the relentless challenge of assignments that stretched my intellect to its limits.

To me, it was supreme—a force not just of empowerment but of transformation. It's almost as if you, the reader, are tempted to skim these pages as one might casually flick through the Bible—seeking a flash of inspiration but unwilling to linger long enough to wrestle with the gravity of the words. Not with the care and reverence of a mother bathing her child, each movement deliberate and imbued with purpose, but with the hurried indifference of someone chasing meaning without committing to its discovery. Why? Because in today's world, there's always something else to rush toward, another distraction pulling us away from depth.

And here lies the heart of the issue—not only in how you may approach this book, but in the very fabric of our modern educational system. The same passive detachment that you might bring to these pages mirrors what dominates our classrooms today, where learning has become a mechanical process, stripped of curiosity and critical engagement.

Once revered as sanctuaries of intellectual growth and transformation, schools have now devolved into mere holding pens for students, where creativity is suppressed, ambition is dampened, and the pursuit of excellence is sacrificed on the altar of mediocrity. Today's educational system appears less a crucible for thinkers and visionaries and more a conveyor belt churning out individuals ill-equipped for the intricate demands of a rapidly evolving world.

Classrooms have been reduced to sterile chambers where the lifeblood of curiosity is drained, and knowledge is stripped to its skeletal remains. Educators, constrained by systemic shackles or depleted of their initial fervor, deliver content that neither challenges the mind nor nourishes the spirit. The result is a generation fed on the intellectual equivalent of empty calories—a diet that neither fortifies their understanding of the world nor prepares them to transcend its challenges.

We were promised enlightenment. Instead, we find ourselves in the midst of a disillusionment, a mass production of cynics whose potential is dulled by the very system that was meant to refine it. The lofty ideals of education—to create thinkers, dreamers, and innovators like the Elon Musk or Richard Branson of our time—have given way to a dispiriting mediocrity.

The pursuit of excellence has been replaced by an assembly-line mentality, where conformity trumps creativity and stagnation masquerades as progress. The consequences of this failure are profound, rippling far beyond the walls of any classroom. We are not merely neglecting to prepare young minds for the complexities of life; in many cases, we are actively undermining their capacity to contribute meaningfully to society. When reason is reduced to shallow thinking, when passion is extinguished by apathy, and when the sacred pursuit of knowledge is recast as a tedious obligation, we are left with a generation that has been betrayed by low expectations and empty promises.

This is not just an educational crisis; it is a philosophical reckoning. Education, in its truest form, is the art of drawing out the latent brilliance in every individual, of empowering them to grapple with the mysteries of existence and emerge with clarity and purpose. We have surrendered this ideal to a hollow, utilitarian framework—one that reduces education to a mechanical process, a means to an end rather than an exploration of the human spirit. In doing so, we have betrayed more than just our children; we have compromised the very essence of what it means to be human, sacrificing curiosity, creativity, and the profound search for meaning on the altar of efficiency and conformity.

Outside my window, the snow falls steadily, blanketing the world from morning to afternoon into a pristine, tranquil landscape. The once-familiar sight of red cars now seems altered, their vibrant hues muted beneath the soft, white duvet of winter. Even the usual purr of passing vehicles is subdued, softened by the steady descent of snowflakes, as if the world itself has quieted, pausing for an annual meditation. The street feels emptier, more contemplative—this Saturday, time itself seems to slow, as the snow invites stillness and introspection into the day.

Immediately, I begun to contemplate the ad hoc shift from autumn to winter, my thoughts were unexpectedly interrupted by a wonder woman's eager voice. Her curiosity is palpable, and she prompts me to recall my first reaction to snow many years ago. Her question, seemingly innocent, double-crosses an expectation of wide-eyed awe, of youthful joy upon encountering a new season, new experiences. She listens assiduously, anticipating some sort of revelation —a tale of wonderment that one associates with the innocent glee of the first snowfall. In her eyes, the snow is magical, a thing to be marveled at, celebrated even, even though it's not brand new to her. But my response is far from the enchanted reverie she expects. "Honestly," I tell her, "My first reaction back then was to check the fridge."

I pause for a moment, sensing her confusion. "You see, the forecast had predicted a full day of snow, and I wanted to make sure I had enough food to last. The last thing I wanted was to brave the cold for groceries or to risk ordering Uber Eats, only to have breakfast arrive colder than the snow outside." Her initial shock quickly turns into bemusement, as if unable to reconcile my response with the childlike awe she had anticipated. She presses on, probing deeper: "Well, what would make you go wow, then?" I chuckled, recognizing her desire for something grand, something extraordinary. "The raw power of a hurricane's fury," I begin. "The violent tremors of an earthquake like it unfortunately happened in Japan at the start of 2024 specifically about 43 kilometers northeast of Anamizu, the kind that pushes human endurance to the brink."

"The devastation of flooding that displaces millions, like the floods in Pakistan, or lightning cracking the sky above jagged peaks in a flash of pure, chaotic energy. The eruption of volcanoes, with molten lava spilling from the Earth's core, or perhaps an asteroid striking the planet, rewriting history with its cataclysmic power. Those are the moments that make me say wow. Those are the true spectacles of nature." Her expression softens, as if contemplating the depth of my words. Snow, in contrast, though, serene doesn't provoke the same visceral reaction. Its beauty is quiet, delicate, and gentle. It's a marvel, no doubt, but one that seems to lose its luster with time, especially when viewed through the lens of human history.

The real shift in human consciousness comes from our ability, and our need, to seek out greater and more complex experiences. It's not that I no longer appreciate the beauty of snow or that I am incapable of marveling at nature's simpler wonders; living in a world constantly confronted by overwhelming forces that challenge our very existence, where the boundaries of our knowledge and understanding are disfigured wonderful moments of quiet and stillness which should be golden is preferred to not be around because my car, or perhaps the Tesla I have been dreaming of, (not Jaguar, they stopped doing cars) rest dormant beneath the snow's heavy embrace, awaiting the inevitable servicing that comes with the change of season. And when that time arrives, the technician often is inadequate of the precision and skill required to address the issue properly.

And so, week after week, I may find myself draining my resources on minor, repetitive repairs—each one a small but persistent reminder of a system that consumes my time and money, leaving me no closer to true peace or resolution. This same duality plays out on a global scale, where the shifting aspirations of individuals—especially in the developing world —mirror this longing for something bigger, something that promises a future beyond the ordinary. Many young people in Africa and Southeast Asia, for instance, now see a visa to the West as their ticket to success, rather than the pursuit of advanced degrees or academic achievement in their home countries.

The dream of a PhD, remarkable flagship of academic and intellectual achievement, seems increasingly secondary to the allure of a life in the West, where opportunities, resources, and a perception of progress are seen as limitless. This trend is as telling as it is troubling. It illustrates a deep-seated dangerousness with the root cause. People are avoiding schools, not out of rebellion, but out of resignation—resignation to the reality that, for many, the education system has become an untrustworthy, broken institution.

The tangible hope for the future no longer resides in academic success, but in geographic relocation. Most suburban fathers no longer speak of the value of learning but of visas— visas to escape to the West. We see this not only in developing nations but in the discontent brewing in wealthier regions as well.

Many adults walking the streets today are, in essence, grown infants—equipped with nothing but the basic tools for survival, but devoid of the intellectual rigor and curiosity once nurtured by education. They are the byproducts of a system that have traded critical thinking for conformity, creativity for efficiency, and intellectual curiosity for rote memorization and despite its vast resources, failed to prepare humanity for the complexities of the world. Millennials have become, for all intents and purposes, intellectual chiffons—light, airy, low IQ and ephemeral, unable to fix simple challenges in their adult lives.

Some members in the Department of

Education in the UK appears to have shifted its focus, prioritizing feelings over fostering intellectual rigor. The human mind is a wellspring of untapped potential. But the kind of intellectual nourishment needed to develop resilience, foresight, and the ability to navigate an increasingly complex world has been denied them. Instead, they've been fed the empty calories of surface-level knowledge, leaving them unprepared for the murkier questions of life, let alone the practical and philosophical problems that require nuanced thinking and hard-earned wisdom.

The story of Moses offers a powerful allegory for what education once was and what it has the potential to become. Moses, an orphaned boy raised in Pharaoh's palace, was shaped by two contrasting worlds: the intellectual opulence of Egyptian learning and the raw, untamed challenges of the wilderness. His life is a narrative of growth, leadership, and transformation—qualities that contemporary education, in its diluted form, increasingly fails to cultivate. Moses was not merely schooled in the knowledge of his time; he was deeply embedded in the philosophy and science of Egypt, then considered the epicenter of civilization. For a reason or two, his education was incomplete until he left the palace and confronted the wilderness—a place where the formal learning of the court was tested against the unforgiving realities of life.

The wilderness honed his resilience, sharpened his instincts, and deepened his capacity to lead. Moses became a leader because his education was transformative, not transactional. He did not merely acquire knowledge; he absorbed wisdom and learned to act decisively in moments of crisis. Today, we are raising generations who never leave Pharaoh's palace—individuals who may know the mechanics of governance but have no sense of the human heart or the magnitude of moral responsibility. Curricula are stripped of complexity, and students are handed participation trophies instead of being challenged to earn their achievements. Syllables are reduced. Specialists who are lost without a working GPS are seethed. Today, precedence is enthroned in the prioritization of the accumulation of credentials over the cultivation of character. Schools churn out graduates who are technically proficient but lack the vision and moral compass to lead. Sinisterism ideas that education is a scam and there is no room for everyone on the planet earth, an idea that already failed with Malthus at the beginning of the 19th century are been ushered.

From Cardiff to Brunei to Derby, universities in the modern era of the great UK have embraced an ideological shift and now focus increasingly on agendas that prioritize the teaching of gender reassignment and identity politics over timeless disciplines.

Transgender policewomen are sanctioned to conduct searches on young girls within campus grounds- —a policy that raises profound questions about privacy, safety, and the boundaries of inclusivity. This evolution is emblematic of a broader societal shift, where the ideals of inclusivity and progressiveness sometimes overshadow foundational principles of fairness, meritocracy, and rational discourse.

Throughout my life, I have been privileged to witness the synopsis the transformative power of education through the lives of remarkable individuals. Dad and mom had been steadfast pillars in shaping my path, two other figures— Kwame Pianim and Mr. Augustine Addo—stand as towering anecdotes to how education had the power not only to transform personal destinies but also redefine the possibilities for entire communities. Kwame Pianim, born in 1940 in Ghana's Bono Region, emerged from a time when education was a rare privilege, reserved for the few, particularly under the constraints of colonial rule. His connection to my family is a deep one—his mother was a sister to my paternal grandfather.

My grandfather, a man ahead of his time, understood the profound importance of education. Defying societal norms that often-left girls uneducated and boys confined to limited opportunities, he ensured every child in the family, regardless of gender, was enrolled in school. This act of foresight set Pianim on a path to greatness. With unyielding determination, he excelled in a system that was only just beginning to take shape. Over the decades, Pianim became a symbol of reform and resilience, building a career as a technocrat committed to good governance and economic progress. His tenure was marked by an unflinching dedication to accountability, even at great personal cost, including imprisonment during turbulent political times. Pianim's life is an indication to the enduring power of education to forge leaders who prioritize justice and progress over personal gain.

Similarly, the story of Mr. Augustine Addo is one of extraordinary achievement forged from humble beginnings. Born in a village so remote that it doesn't appear on any map, Addo grew up surrounded by red-clay huts and bamboo structures, far removed from the trappings of modern life. He is the son of the woman who raised my mother after she was orphaned at a young age. His rise from such obscurity to prominence is a poignant monument to the transformative power of education—it's remarkable ability to shatter barriers, unlock untapped potential, and rewrite the paths of entire lives. Despite such unassuming origins, Addo was given the gift of education, a gift that would prove to be the turning point in his life.

Through unrelenting effort and dedication, he ascended the ranks of academia and professional excellence. His journey saw him become the director of the Institute of Chartered Accountants and later the head of Ghana's Securities and Exchange Commission. he continues to serve on important diplomatic missions, driving initiatives designed to strengthen Africa's banking sector and foster economic stability across the continent. His journey is not just one of personal triumph, but a shining example of pedagogy if not made woke like today elevates and brings life. These close stories of Kwame Pianim and Augustine Addo are powerful testaments to the trailblazing and innovative potential of education, but they are tinged with a sense of profound loss and despair in the current world.

The system that once nurtured such brilliance and propelled individuals from humble beginnings to national prominence is no longer what it used to be. Today, education has lost much of its power as the great equalizer it once was. It has become fragmented and uninspiring, a conveyor belt where many students wander aimlessly, uncertain of why they are even there or what they are meant to achieve.

In the muffed but functional interludes of my time on the revolutionary campus of KNUST, on the western coast of Africa, it was these moments between classes—the casual but exquisite conversations—that truly made the university experience come alive. Whether it was in the main Prempeh Library's break rooms or the impromptu deviated pep talks that preceded group discussions at the at the engineering faculty's summer canopy or walking the familiar paths of Mecca Road to Katanga Hall (*"the university within, the university", "the hall of gentlemen"*) or gathering in and around Anarosa TV room at Ayeduase during Premier League or LaLiga matches and those electrifying UEFA Champions League nights—a recurring question would inevitably emerge in my conversations with friends and familiar faces. These were the spaces where idle chatter turned to remuneration, where casual talk morphed into questions of greater depth.

One afternoon, as we appeared from our rooms to converge and watch football with snacks, the heartbreaking news of Kobe Bryant, his daughter Gianna, and the seven others who perished in the helicopter crash on January 26, 2020, reached us, and everything changed. What had started as a typical weekend—filled with football debates, discussing stats, Ronaldo and Messi—was abruptly overshadowed by the devastation.

The mood shifted instantly, and even those who were not particularly NBA fans sensed the full impact of the loss. The rest of the day was spent in sober, as the magnitude of the tragedy sank in, a somber recollection of how fragile life can be.

My friends and I would confer the future, and with it, the purpose of our education. What were we truly here for? What was the meaning behind the years spent in classrooms, reading texts and passing exams?

The sincerest answers I received were as varied as the people themselves—each person carrying their own set of aspirations, doubts, and societal pressures. In spite of these differences, a singular truth emerged: for many of us, education had become little more than an obligation, a process to be endured alternatively to embrace with purpose. We were not walking a clear path, but multiple variants of seesawed and drifted pipelines, navigating through the motions without any deeper sense of direction. It struck me as a curious paradox: young minds, capable of so much potential, moving through a system that was supposed to unlock their purpose, however so often leaving them lost in the labyrinth of uncertainty.

There were no guiding principles to help us connect the dots between what we were learning and the lives we hoped to build. Amidst these informal discussions, I came to a profound realization: our questions—often brushed off and met with freeze response and associated with voidness and extreme fear concerns of youth—were far from trivial and voluntary exploration. They were the reverberations of a much larger philosophical dilemma: What is the true purpose of education in a world that is ever-changing, where the ground beneath us is constantly shifting?

The modern system still operates on a framework established centuries ago, strategic in its confrontation, oppressive platforms structured and stimulated to produce obedient, compliant workers rather than independent thinkers and physiologically transformed humans. This model finds its roots in the Prussian military of the 1800s, where the objective was to train soldiers who could follow orders without hesitation, undeterred by the rapid changes in the world around us, this outdated construction has stubbornly remained in place and replicated in the elicitation of current institutional walls, sandwiched in this activation chain of dead iceberg woke body and mind syndrome.

From the mighty Amazon River in Brazil, whose serpentine path weaves through the heart of the world's largest rainforest, nurturing an ecosystem teeming with life and mystery, to the Dinaric Alps of Bosnia and Herzegovina, where rugged peaks rise as silent witnesses to the complex history and resilience of a land shaped by empires, war, and renewal, to the twin islands of Trinidad and Tobago, renowned for their booming energy industry, calypso music, and the pulsating rhythms of its carnival traditions; imagine a disingenuous polarized classroom where the vibrant spark of youthful curiosity is gradually extinguished and smothered by the heavy hand of ideological conformity.

At the front of the theatre stands a female teacher, not as a guide to discovery, but as a purveyor of a rigid narrative, whose kids aren't part of the audience. The curriculum, crafted not to inspire critical thinking but to impose a predetermined worldview, focuses relentlessly on critical race theory and the dogma of systemic oppression. In this space, the child is no longer an eager seeker of knowledge but a passive recipient of ideological conditioning, their potential stifled by the narrow confines of a singular perspective. Fueled by academic movements that view the world exclusively through the lens of power dynamics, they have replaced the complexity of human experience with the simplicity of victim and oppressor.

The classroom, once a sanctuary for critical thought, has become a battleground where history is weaponized and children are taught to either bear the burden of collective guilt or embrace a sense of perpetual grievance. Children naturally connect with each other, unbothered by differences.

They share toys, form alliances over the mutual hatred of vegetables or crayons, and find joy in the simplicity of being young. But this curriculum teaches them to categorize, to assess every interaction by its historical baggage rather than its human value. Friendships are strained under the physiological belongings of privilege checks, and innocent questions become potential microaggressions. This focus on race and identity eclipses other essential lessons.

The child who could have learned to marvel at the genius of Newton's laws of motion or the wonder of ecosystems in Antarctica or the chemical combination of molecules of carbon, oxygen and hydrogen to produce ethanol is instead schooled in the perpetual grievance industry. Mathematics becomes a tool of oppression; literature, a showcase of systemic injustice. The world is shrinking to a grim narrative where everyone is either oppressed or an oppressor, leaving little room for innovation, resilience, or the sheer joy of dopaminergic discovery.

Progress has slowed to a turtle crawl as societies become mired in an endless cycle of cultivating cultural impressions where the loudest voices drown out reason, blameworthiness is currency, division is policy and performative virtue-signaling is the new lipophilic wings that controls gene expressions and gender orientations. Picture a kid in the common world entering adulthood, armed with the knowledge of all systemic injustices since the fall of the Roman Empire but incapable of budgeting for groceries or understanding compound interest.

It's as if this receptive system handed them a sword for a battle long finished, leaving them defenseless in the very real struggle to succeed in a complex, competitive world. A parasympathetic generation programmed to see themselves not as architects of possibility but as amplified prisoners of their identities, consumed by energy drinks and neurochemical algorithms with a greater degree of multitudes of disastrous implications concurrently the solution is right in front of apex predatory wolves that targets larger preys surgically and airborne.

CHAPTER ELEVEN:

LEGACY MEDIA IS THE ARMAGEDDON

*"Therefore, putting away falsehood,
let every one of you speak
the truth with his neighbor
for we are members one of another."*
Ephesians 4: 25

N estled in the heart of Scotland's largest city, the Glasgow Subway is a delightful oddity. As one of the smallest subway systems in the world, it offers a unique mix of charm and practicality. Beginning at Partick Station, where the procession of the morning commute mingles with the crisp chill of a Glasgow winter. The station itself is an intersection of eras, with modern ticket barriers standing alongside architecture that hints at the city's industrial heritage. The platform is a mix of subdued grays and weathered tiling, softened by the occasional vibrant orange of the subway's branding.

As the train pulls in, its compact form reminds me of its unique place in the subway world—one of the smallest systems of its kind. Boarding the second-generation stock is an act of mindfulness for anyone of notable height, like myself. The phrase "Mind the Gap" which appeared in the invitation extended to the public for the coronation event of King Charles III in May, 2023 is plastered on the floor along with its counterpart of "Mind Your Head" which is layered on the shallow canopy. I am confidently tall. The low ceilings demand a deliberate duck of the head, a small bow to the quirks of this charming system. Once inside, the geometric design of the seat markers immediately draws the eye. They're like tiny works of art, with angular patterns that evoke a mid-century aesthetic.

The footstools, conveniently tucked beneath the seats, offer a surprising luxury for weary legs—a thoughtful detail often absent in larger, more utilitarian transit systems. As the train lurches forward, the familiar circular motion begins. The subway's nickname, "The Clockwork Orange," comes to mind, a moniker born of its iconic orange trains and circular route. The ride is smooth but intimate—the proximity of the passengers a reminder of just how compact these trains are. Moving past Kelvinhall and Hillhead, the heart of the city's West End, the atmosphere inside the carriage is one of quiet anticipation. Morning commuters clutch their coffee cups or scroll through their phones.

The subtle vibrations of the train are accompanied by the rhythmic clatter of the tracks beneath. At the next station, a fleeting power cut plunges the carriage into near darkness, an oddly common occurrence that never fails to highlight the subway's old-world charm. It's in these moments that the design of the carriage truly shines—brushed steel handrails catching the faint emergency lights, browned leather seat tops offering a warm, tactile comfort, and the perfectly contoured seats harmonizing with the laminate flooring beneath. The 1980s color palette, a subdued symphony of browns and oranges, ties it all together with a retro elegance.

The train continues past Cowcaddens and Buchanan Street, edging closer to the city's core. The sound of the traction motors rises and falls like the inhale and exhale of a mechanical beast, a rhythmic companion to the journey. The subway car itself feels alive, its aged but enduring body carrying generations of Glaswegians through their daily lives. Finally, the train pulls into St. Enoch Station, the end of the line for me this morning. The platform here has its own character—slightly brighter and buzzier than others, as if echoing the energy of the city center above. Tramping off the train, I take a moment to glance back at the departing carriage and witness a quick and efficient changeover unfold.

The driver emerges from the cab, clad in a crisp blue uniform that quietly signifies their role. The material, designed for both pragmatism and professionalism, reflects the dual demands of focus and endurance their work requires. With a smooth, practiced motion, they secure the controls and retrieve the vital key that signifies the handover. This changeover is more than routine—it's a ritual of efficiency. A simple nod or a brief word is exchanged between colleagues, a silent acknowledgment of their shared purpose. The outgoing driver casts a final glance over the cab, their movements deliberate and assured, before stepping onto the platform. Its final farewell comes in the form of an electrical discharge, a faint, sharp thrum that seems almost theatrical—a punctuation mark on its timeless performance.

From here, it's a short walk into the heart of the city. As I step out of the station, the sharp Glasgow air wraps around me, a bracing contrast to the warmth of the subway. The streets are already alive with the early hustle of workers, shoppers, and the city's ever-present pilgrimages. People move with purpose, weaving through Argyle Street like hunters pursuing their morning routines, their energy reminiscent of a colony of ants. Passing the stately Bank of Scotland building, its architecture is a composed stoicism of the city's storied financial history; I find myself immersed in a blend of old and new Glasgow.

The street ahead manicures both crispy modern commerce and the harsh realities of urban life. Continuing my walk, I decide to stop by Tim Hortons, drawn by the promise of a French Vanilla to-go. The café's warmth offers a brief respite as I wait, the rich aroma of freshly brewed coffee mingling with the sounds of orders being called out. Cup in hand, I step back into the brisk morning air, merging once more with the flow of the street. Beneath the towering bridge of Glasgow Central Station, a small community of homeless individuals gathers. Some sit quietly with reusable coffee cups serving as begging bowls, their expressions a mix of resignation and faint hope. Others, still wrapped in blankets, remain motionless, not yet stirred from their uneasy sleep.

Within reach, a few puff early-morning joints, their accents faint and flamboyant in the smooch air. At the far edge of this underpass, a small queue forms for a local food stamp program—an unspoken acknowledgment of the city's ongoing struggles. Most in line are locals, faces hardened by circumstance, but there are a few immigrants too, their unfamiliarity with the city evident in the way they glance around, seeking familiarity.

Just outside the west entrance of Glasgow Central Station, I spot a familiar figure. An elderly man sits at his usual spot, his saxophone resting on his lap. The melody he plays is light but soulful, weaving through the noise of the city like an echo from another time. Rumors suggest he's been playing here for nearly 20 years, his presence as much a part of the station as the commuters who pass by daily. His music is both a marker of continuity and a quiet defiance against the ever-changing cityscape.

As I approach the roundabout near the Motel One Hotel, its grand façade a strikingly gargantuan shape to the modest businesses that flank it, I pause for the traffic. The rhythm of the city—the interplay of elegance and struggle, history and progress—feels particularly vivid here. With my coffee warming my hands, I prepare to face the day, carrying these fragmented impressions of Glasgow with me like snapshots in motion.

On any given workday, during the customary preliminary break in the canteen on the fourth floor of my office building, I find myself enveloped in the quiet rhythm of morning routines. The cafeteria, modest in its design still inviting, offers the simple comforts of both cold and hot drinking water from its reliable pipes —an unassuming but necessary touch. A basket of bananas and apples sits invitingly on the counter, their natural vibrancy a gentle contrast to the sterile hum of office life. in the vicinity, rows of cereal and morning grains stand neatly arranged in their vacuum flasks, their warmth a quiet promise of nourishment and the start of a brief respite from the demands of the day. In this calm, almost ritualistic space, colleagues drift in and out, some in search of a quick refreshment, others simply taking a moment to unwind.

Conversations spark—brief exchanges, normally about the small things, but occasionally evolving into more thoughtful discussions that echo the pulse of the office itself. It's a place where routine and Austria-reflection intertwine, where the simplicity of the moment offers a reprieve, and where, in the midst of the busyness of the day, small connections are made over a cup of coffee or a piece of fruit. On the walls of the canteen, a curated history of the company and its employees is displayed—photos capturing milestones, awards, and moments of achievement that reflect the collective journey of the organization.

Above, flags from various nations hang from the ceiling, a quiet but powerful symbol of inclusion, signaling the global diversity that enriches the workplace. At one end of the room, freezers spin quietly on their axis, stocked with cold treats, while vending machines line the wall, offering quick bites for those in need of a brief escape from their routine. One day, I found myself in the midst of a rather interesting exchange. The conversation spins out between me and two colleagues—one from Wales, the other from Pakistan. We talked about all sorts of things: special interests, rugby, football, and the cities we've each visited. One of them has just returned from South America, the other from Puerto Rico, so you can imagine the travelling stories bouncing around like a ping-pong match. But this particular conversation takes a turn for the curious, and it's one I won't soon forget.

It's months after the UK general elections, and only a few weeks before the upcoming US presidential election. Naturally, the subject of Donald Trump comes up. One of them casually claims that he's a criminal and should be locked up. "Oh, really?" I ask, half expecting a detailed explanation. I'm met with a surprisingly matter-of-fact response: "Well, that's what they're saying on BBC and CNN. He's a threat to democracy." No hesitation, no room for debate. It's as if the decision has already been made, and they've taken it on faith. Now, I consider myself an inquisitive person, so I press further. "So, you're just going with whatever the media says, no questions asked?" And then it hits me. Their response is almost deadpan: "Yeah, pretty much. You know, like the weather or the holidays in the UK. If it's on the news, it's final." And there I am, standing in the breakroom, wide-eyed, trying to process this revelation.

The audacity! These are grown adults, fully capable of independent thought, yet they're swallowing the media's narrative like a buffet breakfast of hot takes and half-baked opinions. And for a moment, I find myself wrestling with disbelief and mild rage. The fact that they've adopted this media-fed worldview without question, and in such a casual manner, makes my blood boil. It's like I'm watching the legacy media function as a giant spin machine, churning out disinformation like it's nobody's business. The real kicker?

The confidence with which they believe it. Forget critical thinking; in their minds, the media has already decided what's true—and that's good enough for them. As a result, my break is anything but relaxing. Instead, I'm left fuming silently, wondering how we've gotten to a point where people take media narratives as gospel, all while I stand there, the last bastion of reasonable skepticism, shaking my head in disbelief. I guess in the world of "unquestionable" news, I'm the odd one out.

A similar exchange happens with my friend Sam, a PhD student in cardiovascular studies at the University of Glasgow. Over the past year, Sam has undergone a jaw-dropping transformation, going from a standard academic to a full-on bodybuilder, muscles rippling as though they were carved out of marble. He's as sharp as a tack, the kind of person whose intellect is not only matched by his commitment to the gym but consistency in all things. With dreadlocks bouncing and a vibrant personality to match, Sam's presence in any conversation is felt before he even speaks.

On this particular day, we're chatting about the usual topics—life, work, the world's endless drama—but as it often does, the conversation takes a sudden turn. We're talking about the growing trend of social media censorship in the UK, a topic that's become more and more pressing. We both agree that the UK seems to be edging dangerously close to a police state, where every word, every post online is scrutinized, and people are held accountable for things they say on social media.

Tommy Robinson, for instance, has been locked up for 18 months—part of it because of a post. The whole situation is enough to make anyone's head spin. Then Sam, in his typical no-nonsense manner, drops a bombshell: "Well, it has to be done. People need to be censored about what they post on social media." My eyelid nearly crashed the floor. I'm staring at him, trying to process the words. This is Sam, the guy who can break down a cardiovascular study in seconds, but here he is, advocating for the kind of censorship I thought we both would be against. I'm stunned—genuinely stunned. My mind races as I try to wrap my head around this sudden shift.

How could Sam, of all people, support such a thing? The very notion of censorship, of silencing individuals based on their online posts, feels like a slap in the face to everything I believe about free speech. Here, he is, calmly justifying it, his muscles tense not from the gym, but from a strange new conviction I didn't see that coming. It's as though we have stumbled onto a different planet.

One where freedom of expression is being traded for "security" or "order," and where even the brightest minds can, at times, fall into the trap of authoritarian thinking. It's a conversation that leaves me shaken, not because of its content, but because of how quickly the tide of opinion can shift—even among the people you'd least expect. And I find myself questioning: If Sam, the critical thinker, can fall for this logic, what hope is there for the rest of us?

The legacy media I grew up with has undeniably undergone a profound transformation, and I am afraid, it's not for the better. I often find myself reminiscing about the evenings when my father would call me to join him for the 7 o'clock news on the Ghana Broadcasting Corporation (GBC). This simple ritual held deeper significance, one that resonates with me to this day. There were, on the surface, two primary reasons for this habit, but beneath them lay two more deepest, almost philosophical motivations.

Seated on the surface like water lily, it was about staying informed, keeping abreast of current affairs—an essential practice for engaging with the world and understanding the events that shape our collective existence. But there was more to it than mere information gathering. Watching the news was also a means of mastering language—specifically, the art of speaking refined, articulate English.

In a society where English language was not merely a tool for communication but a marker of intellect and social standing, this practice felt indispensable. It was about more than just speaking well; it was about wielding language as a magnitude of one's capacity to think, to engage, and to navigate the complexities of the world.

Deeply rooted and hidden like a Russian submarine were far more profound, shaping the way I would come to understand the role of media in society. My father's guidance was not merely about staying informed; he advised me to pay close attention to how the presenters conducted themselves. It was about observing how they mastered their body language, how they looked directly into the camera with unwavering poise, and how they spoke with an authority that exuded truth and confidence.

In this, he imparted a lesson far beyond the content of the news—it was a lesson in dignity. I learned how to present myself with gravitas, how to speak with conviction, and, perhaps most importantly, how to command respect without ever uttering a word. The news, in my father's eyes, was not just a broadcast; it was an art form —one in which integrity was the cornerstone.

The presenters embodied a sense of purpose and professionalism that was palpable, their unwavering commitment to truth shining through their every word. They weren't merely reporting; they were curators of the national spirit, capturing the essence of a collective identity with each broadcast. The way they presented the news wasn't simply about relaying facts; it was about maintaining an unapologetic adherence to truth, without embellishment or fear. The media of those early years was a far cry from what we see today.

There was no censorship—at least, not in the way we understand it now. The news, in all its raw honesty, was what it was. There was no sensationalism, no spin, just the truth, plain and simple. And, perhaps more importantly, it was healthy media. It didn't just inform; it nurtured a sense of community. The faces you saw on the screen—whether it was the news anchors or the hosts of popular programs—became role models for many of us. They were the people we looked up to, the ones we imagined ourselves becoming one day. There was a certain gravitas to them, an almost untouchable quality that made the media feel like something sacred, something you could trust. Whether I was watching TV3, Al Jazeera, or the Financial Times, it followed like a golden age.

There was an excitement in the air, a sense of anticipation when the news came on. You never knew what was going to happen next, but you were sure it would be real, it would be important, and it would shape the way you understood the world. The media wasn't just for entertainment; it was a tool for education. It brought communities together, united by the common thread of shared information.

The news wasn't merely about what's happening in far-off places; it was about us. The tech companies, those early trailblazers of mobile technology, would later tap into this rich well of information. They'd build small computers that fit in your pocket, providing you with daily updates and news feeds wherever you went.

The media had a hand in shaping this new, connected world—one where information was as much a part of our daily lives as the air we breathe.

Whether it was a historian delving into the profound stories of the beaches of Normandy, recounting the harrowing events of war, or exploring the devastating impact of beriberi on malnourished children in Africa, the narratives were always lucid.

From the scientific breakthroughs unfolding in the depths of the Atlantic Ocean to the vibrant, chaotic streets of Modi's Mumbai, each session was told with clarity, drawing connections between the world's most significant struggles and triumphs. Somewhere along the way, the once sacred bond between the media and the public began to unravel. What was once a dependable source of truth, a trusted pillar in society, has gradually transmuted into a battlefield of competing narratives.

The sonorous of it has been obscured by layers of distortion, and in its wake, trust has eroded, leaving behind a fragmented landscape of disinformation. The role models I once admired, those whose voices carried the weight of integrity, have been replaced by a new breed of talking heads. Their credibility, once unassailable, has been diluted, compromised by the relentless commotion of sensationalism that now dominates the media landscape.

The purity of journalism, where facts were presented with dignity and responsibility, has been drowned in the cacophony of clickbait, algorithms, and partisan spin. Today, news is less about conveying truth and more about stoking division, capitalizing on controversy, and capturing allegiance attention. The integrity that once defined the media has been lost in the noise, leaving us with little more than a series of distractions, each vying for our momentary focus.

In today's media landscape, the question has evolved beyond *what* is being said to *who* is saying it, and more critically, *why* they are saying it. The once-clear distinction between fact and opinion has become increasingly obscure, leaving us to navigate a world where truth is no longer anchored, but is instead swept along by the whims of those who control the narrative. The solid foundation that once underpinned the media—where information was presented with integrity and purpose—has given way to a fragile construct, easily toppled by grandstanding aggrandizement and agendas. That media of my youth, the one I watched with my father, seems like a distant memory now, overshadowed by the endless noise of modern-day media.

The debut of audio media was a groundbreaking moment in the evolution of communication. With less than 30 percent of the world's population inclined to sit down and engage with a book or a daily newspaper, listening-based content transformed how information was consumed. It allowed people to multitask while still absorbing knowledge, stories, and ideas—a revolution in accessibility that redefined the electromagnetic landscape. Audio became a trusted medium, anchoring a deeper connection between the speaker and the listener. But now, that trust has been poisoned. It has been contaminated by lies, manipulation, and the relentless push of hidden agendas. The purity of the medium, once rooted in authenticity, has been completely obliterated.

Today, the airwaves are the Syria of deceit, where the promise of clarity has been replaced by confusion. The state of free speech in Brazil has become a flashpoint under the leadership of Luís Roberto Barroso, Chief Justice of the Supreme Federal Court. Many Brazilians are now silenced, wary of expressing opinions that draws scrutiny and the very essence of open dialogue is compromised. This culture of self-censorship extends beyond politics, permeating personal relationships—families fractured, friendships strained, and even marriages dissolved over political allegiances. Journalism, once a revered career path, is increasingly overshadowed by the rise of content creators and social media influencers.

The new arbiters of public opinion are no longer seasoned reporters but everyday citizens with smartphones, live-streaming events or offering commentary. This has democratized access to information, it has also ushered in an epidemic of misinformation, amplified by procedures designed to prioritize untrue statements over substance.

In the UK, petitions to ban children under 16 from using mobile phones reflect mounting fears about the spread of disinformation. Australia, under Prime Minister Anthony Albanese, has already moved to restrict mobile phone use in schools, a step framed as protecting young minds but critiqued as overreach. In this maelstrom free speech, teeters on the edge.

Independent journalists, the watchdogs of society, find themselves under attack—sometimes literally. Without institutional protections, they are ambushed or discredited, their work undermined by those who benefit from controlling narratives. Hate speech and harmful rhetoric have proliferated, fueled by narratives disseminated through certain segments of the media. has increasingly found itself under scrutiny and in decline. In its place, a thriving ecosystem of independent content creation, particularly in the form of podcasts and YouTube channels, has emerged as a preferred alternative. This shift projects not only a malaise with traditional outlets but also a hunger for unfiltered, long-form conversations that delve deeper into complex issues.

Joe Rogan and Tucker Carlson have come to epitomize the rise of a new breed of media personalities who thrive outside the bounds of traditional media. Joe Rogan's *The Joe Rogan Experience* is a flagship example of this transformation. Known for its long-form conversational format, the podcast covers a sweeping range of topics, from health and science to politics and culture, attracting a wide array of guests. Its appeal lies in its unfiltered nature—free from the time constraints and editorial pressures that characterize legacy media.

The podcast's influence spans over 90 countries, with episodes garnering millions of views and listens. Notably, Rogan's recent interviews with high-profile figures such as former U.S. President Donald Trump and tech innovator Elon Musk illustrate its cultural significance. Each of these episodes stretched nearly three hours, a stark contrast to the soundbite-driven exchanges typical of traditional outlets.

Together, they amassed an astounding half a billion views and countless more listens, underscoring Rogan's unique ability to capture public attention on a global scale. Rogan's approach—engaging, in-depth, and often irreverent—offers a stark alternative to the rigid, often superficial narratives of legacy media. His platform serves as a digital town square where ideas are explored with a level of depth and nuance that has become increasingly rare, marking a shift in how audiences consume and interact with media.

Tucker Carlson's transition from traditional cable news to the expansive digital realm has marked a seismic shift in his influence and reach. Once bound by the structural constraints of network television, Carlson has found a new freedom in platforms like X (formerly Twitter), where his content resonates unfiltered and unapologetically. Known for his conservative ethos, Carlson wields this digital platform to spotlight perspectives and voices often excluded or vilified by mainstream outlets. His interviews with global leaders such as Vladimir Putin of Russia, Viktor Orbán of Hungary, and Javier Milei of Argentina demonstrate his commitment to tackling geopolitically charged subjects.

These leaders, often criticized or dismissed in

Western media as authoritarian or extreme, find in Carlson's platform a space to articulate their perspectives directly to an audience that might otherwise never hear them. In these discussions, Carlson circumvents the interpretative lens of legacy media, offering viewers an unmediated look at controversial figures. By doing so, he challenges the entrenched norms of journalistic framing, allowing his audience to draw their own conclusions about complex international issues.

These engagements are not without controversy, as detractors accuse him of providing a platform for divisive rhetoric. Meanwhile, to his supporters, Carlson is redefining the media's role by breaking barriers in political discourse. The emergence of podcasts and platforms like YouTube has sparked a significant shift away from traditional media, engaging broader cultural and social dynamics. In a time when many see traditional outlets as overemphasized, superficial, and increasingly dismissive of critical thought, these newer mediums offer an alternative that feels more authentic. Where once news and narratives were shaped by a handful of powerful institutions, now anyone with a voice and a platform can contribute to the larger conversation.

For young men in particular, this cultural shift takes on deeper significance. Mainstream media has often been critical of what it labels "traditional masculinity," pushing narratives that undermine values once celebrated as pillars of strength, responsibility, and resilience. This shift has left many feeling alienated, as if their identity and values are being actively discouraged or punished. In this context, independent media, with its less controlled, more diverse range of perspectives, becomes a refuge—a space where different ideas can be explored without the fear of being silenced or ostracized. This is more than just a technological shift; it's philosophical and flooded with commonsense. Independent media offers a counterpoint to the homogenized, often polarized views of traditional outlets, allowing individuals to question, explore, and form their own conclusions.

In an era where information is weaponized and ideologies clash, these platforms offer a rare opportunity for open dialogue and intellectual freedom—one that the traditional media establishment struggles to provide. It is a new intellectual frontier, where diversity of thought is not just tolerated, but encouraged, and where old narratives are challenged in favor of a more nuanced, multifaceted understanding of the world. However, the independence of platforms like YouTube or X is not without challenges.

Recent threats of stricter European Union regulations, such as the Digital Services Act, signal attempts to impose greater control over online content. It claims to ostensibly aimed at curbing misinformation, such measures also risk stifling the very freedom of expression that has made these platforms a haven for diverse voices by silencing people with jail terms and slammed with fines. Pavel Durov, the founder of the popular messaging platform Telegram, was arrested on August 24, 2024, at Le Bourget Airport near Paris. The arrest stemmed from an ongoing investigation by French authorities, who have issued multiple allegations against him.

The charges reportedly include serious offenses such as fraud, drug trafficking, cyberbullying, organized crime, and terrorism. However, these accusations center around Telegram's tenacity of offering an encrypted, private space for communication, allowing users to share information freely and failure to moderate contents and resistance to censorship. Content creators now face a delicate balancing act: maintaining their authenticity and navigating the pressures of regulatory oversight.

I have owned and flipped through the pages, and frothily deep- read back-to-back historically great books of the biographies of chronicled figures like John F. Kennedy, Martin Luther King Jr., and Kwame Nkrumah; marked by profound influences on their respective eras. Each of them navigated the treacherous waters of power, race, and politics, and ultimately, each of them was subjected to violent attempts on their lives—efforts that disrupted their visions and reshaped the course of history. Their portraits hang in my room as a testament to their impact on global landscape and airspace and the tragic narratives surrounding their assassinations have become indelible in the collective memory.

JFK's assassination on November 22, 1963, in Dallas, Texas, was a pivotal moment in American and world history. Lee Harvey Oswald, would go down charged with the crime, shot the president from the Texas School Book Depository while Kennedy was traveling in a motorcade. The impact of this event on the nation cannot be overstated—it shattered the sense of stability and optimism that many historians had felt, especially given the hopefulness Kennedy embodied in the early 1960s.

Dr. Martin Luther King Jr., an emblematic figure of the civil rights movement, was also targeted for his role in advocating for racial equality and justice. King was assassinated on April 4, 1968, in Memphis, Tennessee, while standing on the balcony of the Lorraine Motel. James Earl Ray was arrested and convicted for the murder, but like Kennedy's assassination, King's death has been shrouded in controversy and conspiracy. His assassination further deepened divisions in the U.S., especially as the country was already grappling with the tumult of the 1960s, including the Vietnam War and the racial tensions of the Civil Rights movement.

Dr. Kwame Nkrumah, Ghana's first President and a key figure in African liberation, also faced multiple assassination attempts, his ideals of Pan-Africanism and independence challenging not just the colonial powers but also internal political opponents. Though he survived these attempts, Nkrumah's legacy as a champion of African unity and self-determination remains influential to this day.

Four months ago, I witnessed a broad day live assassination attempt on my screen, that hugely captured global attention—the near-death of President Donald Trump in 2024.

On a campaign trail in Butler, Pennsylvania, on July 13th, 2024, while preparing for a public address, Trump became the target of a gunman. As I watched it unfold from my room, what seemed like a routine political event quickly turned into a moment of uncertainty and fear. The stage was set, the crowd was gathered, and then, in an instant, the atmosphere shifted as the gunman took his shot. The rise of divisive ideologies, the amplification of hate speech, and the relentless spread of misinformation majorly by the legacy media have created an environment where further attacks against someone's grandfather have become an all-too-real consequence.

As I mull over and ruminate on the lives of Kennedy, King, Nkrumah, and Trump, I am struck by the profound cost of controlling the narrative. The legacy media, with its powerful influence, has a tendency to shape perceptions, often with dire consequences for those who become the targets of such influence. These figures, each with their own vision and ideals, were not merely attacked for their actions but for the narratives that were constructed around them.

I am enraged because this manipulation of the public psyche, especially through legacy media, has lasting consequences. It doesn't just affect how we view our leaders—it affects how we view each other, leading to a world where conversations are fraught with suspicion, hatred, and distrust. This is the weaponized world we live in today, and but it's not how things are meant to be.

CHAPTER TWELVE:

THE LEAGUE
OF DEBTS AND
NIGHTMARES

*"The rich rules over the poor,
and the borrower is
the slave of the lender."*
Proverbs 22: 7

T here are moments in history when the tide shifts so subtly that the world fails to grasp its significance until the waters have risen too high. The late 1700s and beginning of the 1900s was one such moment—a quiet revolution that redefined the dynamics of power and wealth in the world. Two landmark developments that year—the establishment of the Federal Reserve and the ratification of the legislation introducing the income tax—did not merely adjust the economic landscape. They planted the seeds of a system that would slowly tighten its grip, choking the financial liberty of millions.

Today, we live in the shadow of these twin leviathans, ensnared by a system that siphons the fruits of labor and converts earnings into debt, dependence, and despair. To understand the depths of this systemic theft, we must dissect its mechanisms and the ways it has been normalized. In 1913, the income tax was sold as a modest levy, affecting only the wealthiest few. Politicians assured the public that it was a necessary measure to ensure fairness and fund the government responsibly.

This will quickly change within a generation, the tax would become universal, and its scope expanded far beyond its original intent. The income tax represents more than a revenue stream—it symbolizes a profound shift in the balance of power between individuals and the state. Once implemented, it redefined earnings as property of the government. What citizens keep is not a right but a privilege granted by policymakers.

This inversion of ownership is a breach of faith of economic freedom, turning wage earners into custodians of their own labor, subject to confiscation at the whim of bureaucrats. This categorical situation is as worse as the Terrorism Confinement Center (CECOT), located in Tecoluca, El Salvador - a high-security mega-prison designed to house members of violent gangs, particularly those involved in terrorist activities; has the labyrinthine complexity of the tax code. With its endless deductions, credits, and penalties, it is less a system of fairness than a tool of manipulation. It incentivizes debt and discourages self-reliance, traps small business owners in regulatory quicksand, and punishes those who dare to accumulate wealth outside the approved boundaries.

In this maze, the average citizen is not a participant but a captive. If the income tax is the visible chain, inflation is the invisible one. It is shrouded under the guise of stabilizing the economy like a native Iranian girl with her face glowing with natural beauty, which is partially illuminated by the soft fabric that drapes around her head, with a warm, almond-shaped eyes, framed with lashes that accentuate her gaze and her skin olive-toned or sun-kissed complexion, reflecting the diversity of Arab backgrounds. She may wear minimal makeup, perhaps a bit of eyeliner or soft lipstick, enhancing her features while keeping her look understated.

The Federal Reserve of the United States in 1913 or the Bank of England in the 1700s has institutionalized instability over the period of mankind through the manipulation of interest rates and control of the money supply which has turned currency into a depreciating asset.

Consider this: a pound or a dollar in the early 1900s could buy 20 times what it can today. This erosion is not natural; it is engineered. Inflation is often described as a "hidden tax," but it is more insidious. It rewards debtors—most notably the government and punishes savers. The prudent worker, diligently setting aside money for the future, finds their nest egg diminished in value year after year. Meanwhile, those with access to cheap credit—banks, corporations, and speculative investors—amass fortunes in assets whose values are artificially inflated.

The policies have turned the economy into

a casino, where those who play with borrowed chips win big, while those who play with hard-earned cash are left holding worthless cards. This system is not broken; it is functioning exactly as designed—to extract wealth from the many and concentrate it in the hands of the few. The pillars established in 1913 have enabled the rise of an extraction ecosystem, where every facet of modern life is monetized and leveraged against the individual.

From the steep annual cost of health insurance to the ambiguous terms of car insurance to the premium and unguaranteed returns of life insurance, the promises of a safeguarding packages have become a relentless predator and consume a disproportionate share of income, offering diminishing coverage as a compensation. The average family pays thousands annually for policies riddled with exclusions and loopholes, as insurers rake in record profits.

Housing, once the missing piece of a good life, is now a financial quicksand. Government-backed mortgages and artificially low interest rates have inflated home prices to absurd levels across the globe, forcing families into averagely twenty-year loans that consume half their income. The home is no longer a solid groundswell of stability but a financial trap, where equity growth is dwarfed by the weight of debt and upkeep. Meanwhile, wages have stagnated, failing to keep pace with inflation or the skyrocketing cost of living in the major provinces of many democracies not just in the West but in Southwest Africa and Southeast Asia. Middle income workers are increasingly tethered to corporations not by choice but by necessity, reliant on employer-provided health insurance and pensions that may never materialize.

This is not capitalism; it is neo-feudalism. Workers labor not for themselves but to feed a system that treats them as disposable resources. The most insidious aspect of this economic system lies not just in its operation but in its deep normalization. Over decades, it has woven itself so thoroughly into the fabric of daily life that most people no longer see its mechanisms, only its outcomes. Taxation, inflation, and debt are no longer debated as optional constructs but are treated as immutable laws of nature. This normalization is not accidental but cultivated —through education, culture, and the subtle reinforcement of power structures.

Back in high school chemistry labs or college genetic engineering lecture halls, I wasn't the type to specialize in delivering speeches or running for class president. Instead, I chose to serve in other leadership roles outside the classroom. It was rewarding to contribute my skills to a different group of peers—most of them finishers, with a handful of starters. Of course, whenever a lecturer unexpectedly called on me to answer a question or defend my claims, I responded with composed confidence. I wove my points together with sharp reasoning and vivid illustrations, treating each moment as an opportunity to represent myself with precision and depth. It was my way of protecting my intellectual "brand" and demonstrating my indefatigable will.

My participatory responses always ventured beyond the boundaries of what was expected, sometimes even surpassing the lecturer's imagination with original insights or nuanced perspectives. On other particular days, that the spark of brilliance might have been muted, or when treading an unknown territory like a boma in the wild beast of grasshoppers, I still managed to assemble my thoughts, and defended the standard of engagement and curiosity, knowing that each challenge was a stage to refine my skills and stretch my intellectual limits. I did not place precedence on being heard either.

I only did so when a rule was bend or fabricated at the expense of others. Notable anecdotal report being that the student cannot be late, but when the authority comes in late, we are to get along with it because he's elderly, was engaged in a constructive executive membership meeting or the fact that he is the cousin of superman.

Those of us who dared to ask difficult questions—challenging norms or interrogating the systems we couldn't fully grasp—were often labeled rebels. Our curiosity was mistaken for defiance, and we were branded as arrogant or troublesome, dismissed for questioning the very foundations of what others accepted without a second thought. Both state-owned and private schools, under the guise of financial literacy, don't teach students to question the system's foundations but rather to manage its burdens: how to budget for debt, how to leverage credit responsibly, how to save against the eroding effects of inflation. This isn't empowerment; it's conditioning—training individuals to accept the rules of a game they didn't create.

The legacy media and advertising agencies with their counterfeit promo codes push an aspirational narrative, glorifying consumption and promoting debt as a gateway to happiness and status. Financing a car, a home, or even a vacation is sold as progress, while saving or opting out of the rat race is cast as boring or unambitious. In many anglophone communities, those who dare to rebuttal its very design—are marginalized as radicals or dreamers. They are often met with skepticism, or worse, dismissal, their voices drowned by the prevailing mantra: "This is just the way things are." This narrative isn't just defeatist; it's a tool of control, ensuring that the status quo remains unchallenged by framing alternatives as unthinkable or impractical. This sense of imbalance—of a rigged game—gnaws at the collective psyche.

It has manifested in burnout, in rising mental health crises, in a generational disillusionment with the promises of hard work and meritocracy. Yet, for all this frustration, the tools to challenge the system remain out of reach for many, buried under decades of propaganda that has successfully rebranded systemic inequity as inevitable reality. I have been delving into the apostolical and the epistemological Book of Exodus, a profound narrative of humanity's first recorded journey from tyranny and slavery toward freedom and the pursuit of happiness. It is a story of a people reclaiming their identity and rights, much like the ideals captured in modern frameworks like the Bill of Rights.

The Israelites' escape from Pharaoh's tyranny is a timeless New York Statue of liberation —a breaking of chains both physical and psychological. Revisionist history has shown that liberation often comes with a cruel irony: the visible chains may be shattered, human societies with relentless tendency have replaced overt systems of oppression with subtler, more Machiavellian forms of control. In ancient times, it has been rigid hierarchies or tribal dominance. In modernity, its bureaucracies, economic structures, and cultural narratives that ensure the masses remain tethered to systems that benefit the few at the expense of the many. For a people who had known nothing but servitude, the prospect of freedom was exhilarating, even if the concept was foreign to most. They marched into the wilderness with hope, unburdened by the brutal oppression that had defined their existence.

In the UK, a growing divide has emerged, not necessarily between the rich and poor, but between those who are able to maintain financial stability and those who are overwhelmed by a system that pushes them into a perpetual cycle of debt and stress. It's a quiet crisis that operates beneath the surface of polished smiles and outward success. In cities like Manchester and Nottingham, the image of the successful, happy worker is often a facade masking the mental and financial toll the system exacts.

I recently visited Manchester, a city celebrated for its post-industrial regeneration, with glitzy shops, high-end restaurants, and iconic luxury car dealerships lining its streets. On the surface, it seems many are living the dream: well-dressed professionals with designer bags, residing in upscale apartments or sprawling suburban homes. Yet, beneath this veneer lies a stark reality. According to a recent report by the Office for National Statistics, a staggering number of people in Greater Manchester are living paycheck to paycheck, even as they project an image of wealth and status.

The increase in credit card debt, loans, and the weight of rising inflation are pushing many to the brink. A missed payment on a credit card or loan could easily trigger a cascade of problems, and many people live in constant anxiety about the financial abyss that looms if they fall behind. One example can be found in the cases of local workers who, despite holding steady jobs, are left facing crippling debt due to high interest rates and an unforgiving cost of living. Even a small financial misstep can derail their lives entirely.

Similar issues are evident in Nottingham, where the cost-of-living crisis has hit vulnerable communities particularly hard. Even those receiving state benefits are not shielded from the system's shortcomings. Many struggle to afford basic necessities like food, utilities, and transport, all while living under the constant stress of an uncertain financial future. Despite the government's financial support mechanisms, the gap between the cost of living and available income continues to widen.

In the months following Keir Starmer's election, the UK's political landscape has taken a sharp turn, exposing the undercurrents of disillusionment that many feared. What initially seemed like a bright new beginning after 14 years of Conservative rule has quickly devolved into a narrative of broken promises, unheeded concerns, and a growing desire for change—one that echoes across the country. For millions of citizens and legal residents, Starmer's leadership has felt less like the fresh start they envisioned and more like a continuation of the systemic failures they sought to escape. This mounting frustration has crystallized in an extraordinary moment of collective action: over two million people have signed a petition demanding a reelection.

This is no longer just about policy disputes or political maneuvering; it reflects a deeper crisis of trust, representation, and leadership. Starmer's Labour Party, once heralded as the hope for a fairer and more equitable society, has fallen short of delivering on its most fundamental promises.Farmers, once a key part of Labour's support base, now find themselves alienated by policies that ignore their needs, while working-class citizens watch their expectations fade into the distance.

The very essence of democracy—the idea that political leaders are chosen to reflect the will and needs of the people—seems to have been forgotten. What we are witnessing is a moment of reckoning for the very idea of political leadership in the 21st century.

The political elite, regardless of party, have become so disconnected from the everyday struggles of the citizens they claim to represent that trust has eroded to the point of near irreparability. This is not simply a failure of Keir Starmer or Labour—it's a failure of a system that has bred cynicism, where the promises of change become increasingly hollow as the status quo remains unchallenged.

Though I hold my own reservations about Keir Starmer's leadership, it is particularly concerning to observe the behavior and conduct of some individuals appointed to high-ranking roles under his government. The Foreign Policy Minister, David Lammy, who has shown a propensity for undiplomatic outbursts, including his audacious public disrespect toward U.S. President-elect Donald Trump, stating that, "the people's president is not only a woman hating, neo-Nazi sympathizing sociopath, but also a profound threat to the international order". Alike remarks, regardless of personal views, reflect poorly on the UK's capacity for measured international relations. Diplomacy requires tact, and undermining a key global partner does little to strengthen Britain's standing on the world stage.

The current Chancellor of the Exchequer, Rachel Reeves made history as the first female to hold this position, and also represents Leeds West and has been a prominent person who parties on her off days. She may be as competent as the scoresheet suggests but her policy decisions appear more reflective of a "copy-and-paste" strategy than innovative fiscal leadership, and has since then failed to inspire confidence.

With the economy at a precarious juncture, the lack of originality and foresight in financial management raises serious questions about this administration's ability to navigate the challenges ahead. Philosophically, this moment exposes the fragility of hope in the modern political system. When people vote for change, they do so with the understanding that their lives might improve, that their voices will be heard, and that their leaders will act in accordance with the values that were sold to them. But when those hopes are dashed, when those leaders fail to even make a good-faith attempt at addressing the issues they promised to fix, it's not just a political narcissistic underperforming betrayal—it's an existential diabolical bolus with traces of antisemitism and grandma killer syndrome.

The very belief in the possibility of progress becomes undermined, leaving behind a toxic cynicism that poisons the public's relationship with politics itself. The petition for reelection is not just a call for a new government—it's a plea for meaning in a system that has grown so disjointed and indifferent to the real lives of its citizens. It's a cry for accountability in an age where politicians, like so many institutions, have become detached from the people they serve. In this context, the petition represents not just a political statement, but a philosophical one: a demand for leadership that recognizes the deep, real needs of its people, and for a system that can still deliver on its promises of fairness, opportunity, and dignity.

This is not an endorsement for a political reelection in the UK; it is an appeasement. It is not akin to the Munich Agreement of the 1930s, where British and French leaders—most notably Prime Minister Neville Chamberlain—allowed territorial expansions like the annexation of Austria and the Sudetenland in hopes of averting a larger war with Nazi Germany. Nor is it comparable to the Iran Nuclear Deal finalized on July 14, 2015, after extensive negotiations—a landmark agreement between Iran and the P5+1 nations (the United States, the United Kingdom, France, Russia, China, and Germany), along with the European Union, aimed at ensuring Iran's nuclear program remained peaceful while granting sanctions relief.

Instead, it is a placation—a response to the silent despair etched on the face of a mother who cannot feed her children or afford them slippers. Despite fulfilling her obligations to the farmer, who in turn breaks his promise, she is left with a broken dignity and a profound sense of betrayal.

When most people think of Dubai, their minds often drift to the iconic Burj Khalifa, the sprawling modern airport, or the royal family

—chief among them Sheikh Mohammed bin Rashid Al Maktoum, the current ruler of Dubai and Vice President of the UAE. His leadership has been pivotal in transforming this once modest desert emirate into a dazzling global metropolis.

What truly sets Dubai apart, however, and allows it to defy conventional economic logic, is its tax-free system. Dubai's evolution from a small trading port in the late 20th century to a global financial powerhouse is a testament to calculated ambition and strategic diversification.

In the 1990s, Dubai was still heavily reliant on oil revenues, much like its Gulf neighbors. Yet, the emirate's leaders envisioned a future that extended far beyond oil wells. The real turning point came under the leadership of Sheikh Mohammed bin Rashid Al Maktoum, who ascended to power in 2006 after succeeding his brother. Under his rule, Dubai underwent a sweeping transformation—not just physically, with its striking skyline and world-class infrastructure, but also structurally, through significant investments in infrastructure, real estate, and tourism.

Most notably, the emirate's tax policies spurred a profound economic shift, making Dubai a beacon for global investment and enterprise. As most countries around the world rely heavily on taxes to fund infrastructure, public services, and governmental programs,

Dubai adopted a system that eliminated direct taxation on personal income and most corporate earnings. This was a bold move that directly contradicted the tax-heavy models seen in Western economies.

This tax-free environment was a cornerstone of Dubai's economic model, drawing in foreign investments, multinational corporations, and affluent expatriates eager to escape the heavy tax burdens of their home countries. The ruling family's decision to keep taxes low, if not absent, was a signal to the world that Dubai was open for business, offering opportunities and incentives like few others could. The lack of personal income taxes meant that workers in Dubai could keep nearly all of their salaries—an attraction that lured top talent across industries, from finance and technology to hospitality and healthcare.

Meanwhile, companies operating in Dubai's free zones were largely exempt from corporate taxes, which allowed businesses to thrive in an environment of less financial regulation and more opportunity. Dubai's economy grew exponentially as a result of this policy. The city became a global hub for finance, with international banks setting up regional headquarters. The stock market boomed, and high-profile real estate projects, like the Palm Jumeirah, Burj Khalifa, and the Dubai Marina, brought the world's attention to the emirate.

The tax-free model worked hand-in-hand with an ambitious real estate development strategy, which began in earnest during the early 2000s. Dubai's infrastructure became a magnet for tourists and expatriates, with world-class resorts, luxurious shopping malls, and ever-expanding transportation networks, including the Dubai Metro. Meanwhile it wasn't just tourism and luxury real estate that fueled the Dubai economy. The absence of taxes also encouraged a robust trade and logistics sector. Dubai's geographic location made it an ideal trading hub between the East and West, and the city's ports and logistics networks became some of the busiest and most efficient in the world. Many Gulf nations continue to rely heavily on petroleum as a source of income, Dubai has cultivated industries like finance, tourism, aviation, and real estate, ensuring that its economy is not vulnerable to the volatility of global oil prices.

In 2020, oil made up only about 1% of Dubai's GDP—an extraordinary achievement considering its initial reliance on the energy sector. What is clear is that Dubai's model has created a place where wealth is not just generated—it's cultivated. And the success of Dubai's economy stands as a testament to the idea that sometimes, getting out of the way of business can allow it to flourish in ways that more bureaucratic and heavily taxed systems cannot.

I have a pragmatic and proud cousin, Sarafina, who lives in Kansas City, the hometown of Bill Clinton, the 42nd president of the United States. She is a doctor, a remarkable young mother, and an Assistant Professor in the Department of Anesthesiology, Pain, and Perioperative Medicine at The University of Kansas Medical Center. She is also an anesthesiologist at The University of Kansas Health System.

Sarafina embodies what many perceive as the essence of the Western dream—success, achievement, and upward mobility. After years of rigorous medical school, completing her residency, and marrying the love of her life, Stirling—a recently graduated plastic surgeon —her life appears picture-perfect. She has a beautiful baby boy, a charming home, and a promising future. Her social media feeds are filled with genuine joy: photos of her radiant smile, her baby nestled in love, and occasional gatherings with friends in their 30s and 40s.

However, beneath these snapshots of perfection lies a more complex and sobering reality—a story often left untold. Behind the unfiltered smiles and family portraits looms a staggering debt of nearly half a million dollars. This burden doesn't reflect the traditional economic dream but instead highlights the financial cost of achieving it. Her medical degree alone has saddled her with over a quarter of a million dollars in student loans. Stirling, her husband, faces a similar financial strain from his extensive training as a plastic surgeon. Together, they grapple with an overwhelming mountain of debt, so immense that the path to financial freedom feels uncertain at best.Calculate that to their mortgage and the looming pressure of taxes (with one $40,000 tax bill already paid off only six months ago), and it becomes clear that despite their professional achievements, they are tethered to a system that seems to trap rather than liberate.

The western dream promises that anyone, no matter where they come from, can rise above their circumstances. But for this young Ghanaian-American woman, who has made a life for herself in Kansas, the dream feels increasingly like an elusive myth. She wonders if it's even possible to "make it" in her situation, America, or if the system is rigged to ensure that only a select few get to truly prosper. For someone like her—who has put in the work, endured the sleepless nights, sacrificed everything to get where she is—why does the dream feel so distant? This is not a story about a young woman lamenting the loss of her "dream life." It's a story of a flawed system that, rather than supporting its brightest minds, weighs them down with the very tools they are told to use to succeed. The system isn't just about the burden of student loans or taxes; it's about how those who are supposed to be the future of our society—the ones who heal, educate, and innovate—are left scrambling to survive in an economy that offers them no safety net. And in the end, it's about how the western dream, once a beacon of hope, has become a set of shackles.

In the UK today, the age-old narrative of the "good, satisfactory royal life" rings hollow. For many, especially those in their early twenties or thirties, the belief that hard work and education lead to prosperity has been replaced by a harsh reality: lifelong debt. The promise of a better life through education and loans is an illusion —one that leaves many trapped, burdened by student loans, mortgages, and credit debt. In my neighborhood, the mood is one of resignation, as a degree no longer guarantees success—only crippling debt.

There is a saying in my community: "If you don't borrow, you're invisible." It's a painful truth. Debt has become a prerequisite for participation in the economy—whether it's student loans for a degree or mortgages for a home. But the real cost goes beyond finances; it's emotional and psychological. Those who take on this debt live in constant fear of falling behind. Miss a payment? It could ruin your future. The pressure is suffocating, and for many, the dream of ever getting ahead remains just that—a dream. The saddest part is that, for many, the reality is sinking in: they may never be able to climb out of this hole.ter life—the one that once brought an immigrant like me to these shores and motivated generations like my fathers to work hard—is slipping away. Money has been is a significant factor affecting mental health.

I don't need to quote or reference any article to make my point. Just take a moment to look at the faces of your neighbors or the people on your streets—whether it's a group of churchgoers returning from duty in Coatbridge or late shifters rushing to the bus spots in Central Milton Keynes. The situation is one of hopelessness, with little sense of a future. Ten out of nine people in the lobby of London Waterloo or Edinburgh Waverley train stations seem unhinged, overwhelmed by a barrage of mental struggles. And don't ask me about the algebra—it's not a mathematical error. I was the best student in my core mathematics subjects. From differential vector equations to statistical probabilities to geometric optimization, my academic record was spotless.

The empirical evidence suggests there is a near-certainty of mental distress among these individuals—whether tested or not, including the genetic and embryonic components that shape their futures. The future of their unborn lineage is already set, and there's nothing they can do to change it. They, too, will be strangled by these invisible forces. It's appalling! Threats, depression, and anxiety are merely the starting points of this spiral, while long-term psychological strain becomes the inevitable companion for many. In the same way that everyone at Koko or La Cheetah club is carried away by the night's energy, the storm of mental strain knows no boundary—it doesn't distinguish between a Lamborghini and a Lexus.

I will not document national debts. I refuse to get caught in a cyclical bubble. Be reminded to send an email to the Bulgarian economist Kristalina Georgieva and the International Monetary Fund for data collection. As you should know by now, this is neither an eerie coincidence nor simply a delightfully arranged byproduct of economic mismanagement—it is a glaring indictment of leadership failures. Those entrusted with the reins of governance have fallen prey to the allure of short-term political gains, redirecting resources toward superficial projects that bring fleeting applause but no long-term solutions.This persistent fixation on immediacy over foresight has relegated essential reforms to the sidelines, allowing systemic fiscal challenges to fester.

What remains is a legacy of unfulfilled promises and a mounting, unsustainable financial burden, crafted by the cost of inaction and the astronomical nuances imposed by incumbent leaders on the shoulders of the modern-day dreamer.

CHAPTER THIRTEEN:

EPILOGUE: CAN THE SHOELESS BOY BE PRESIDENT?

"For I know the plans I have for you,
says the Lord,
plans for welfare and not for evil,
to give you a future and a hope."
Jeremiah 29:11

"It is not the critic
who counts;

*not the man who points out
how the strong man stumbles, or
where the doer of deeds could
have done them better.
The credit belongs to the man who
is actually in the arena,
whose face is marred by dust and sweat
and blood; who strives valiantly;
who errs, who comes short again and again,
because there is no effort without
error and shortcoming;
but who does actually strive to do the deeds;
who knows great enthusiasms, the great devotions;
who spends himself in a worthy cause;
who at the best knows in the end the
triumph of high achievement,
and who at the worst, if he fails,
at least fails while daring greatly,
so that his place shall never be with those cold and
timid souls who neither know victory nor defeat."
Theodore Roosevelt: The Man in the Arena.*

Y ou might be wondering what I have left to say in this final chapter after taking you on a cross-continental marathon—a journey as ambitious as Elon Musk's Starship orbiting Earth. Well, if you've come this far and still aren't moved by what's already been shared, then perhaps you are part of the problem. This book isn't for spectators. Pass it on to someone who's ready to act, someone who will take its message and do something constructively meaningful with it. That said, it's never too late to change your mind and join those willing to make a difference. The ball is in your court. Make that executive decision now or it would be made for you.

I have been fortunate in many ways— some privileges succulent, others almost surreal. Growing up in a two-parent household was not just a blessing, it was a mark of distinction, a prestige that many can only dream of. Being introduced to great books by my father is undoubtedly my greatest asset since Napoleon saw his High Seas Fleet scuttled, his overseas trade annihilated, his colonies ordered to bend the kneel. I have mentioned being the fourth child and a first-generation member of my family; on any particular day, my siblings, with their lighter skin and quicker minds, tend to shine brighter. I have picked up something useful among the most of fatal errors.

I'm not here to lecture you about anything; I'm still figuring things out myself. Dr. Jordan Peterson has already covered extensively in his writings. In his books, from *12 Rules for Life* to *Those Who Wrestle with God*, he offers a wealth of guidance on avoiding such missteps. Among these classifications, I had the honor of serving as president of a community organization called *Youth Focus* in the very neighborhood where I grew up in Africa. It wasn't a grand title bestowed by election, nor did it come with power, bureaucracy, or a national treasury to lean on. What I had and always will was passion, ingenuity, and a deep sense of responsibility to the people.

My team (CY, Chris, Elvis, William, James, Latif etc) and I accomplished more during a single summer break from university than the local Member of Parliament—whose home was just ten minutes from the community's struggles—had achieved in years. I'm not here to list our accomplishments or dwell on what could have been done better. But I will say this: we lobbied for clean drinking water, organized football tournaments to raise funds for small startups in the community, and launched a sexually transmitted interactions (STI) awareness campaign that tackled shockingly high infection rates in the community.

Working at a private Muslim hospital in the area, I'd seen the grim numbers—three out of four young girls affected. The urgency was palpable. I also had a conversation with a group of boys-*those* boys, you know the type. Think of a crew straight out of a Leonardo DiCaprio movie, all swagger and mischief. You can picture them already, can't you? But what left the deepest impression on me wasn't the disheartening reality of children drinking from the same stream as their cattle or the morning porridge sellers fetching water from the end of that same polluted source.

It was a conversation I had with a group of boys—roughly aged 7 to 12—who were playing near the roadside. All of them were barefooted. Two of them were shirtless, covered in the omnipresent red dust of the region. One clutched a broken bicycle tire, his companion holding a stick to roll it along. Another boy had a single paracetamol tablet in his hand, tasked by his mother to fetch relief. The last boy stood apart, gripping a dog-eared, dirt-streaked booklet of multiplication tables like it was a treasure. Out of flatness, I asked them about school and what they wanted to be when they grew up.

Their answers were as raw as they were

revealing. One envisioned to be a farmer like his father; another dreamed of becoming a truck driver, following in his uncle's footsteps. The third, with a mischievous grin and a gesture, proclaimed he'd be a gangster—a choice they all found uproariously funny. But it was the final boy who silenced their cackling and guffawing. "I want to be president," he declared, with a confidence that defied his surroundings. The others erupted into teasing giggles, but he stood firm. "I'll fix the roads for my mom," he said, his tone steady, "so when she comes back from the farm, she won't fall and break her ankle again."

In that dusty moment, under the blazing sun, this child divulged the essence of leadership— empathy born of lived experience and the desire to change what's broken, not for himself, but for others. His words carried the flesh and blood imprints of the realization of the people's pain in his young life, more power than the carefully scripted promises of mumbo jumbo politicians. That boy with the multiplication table may or may never grace a ballot paper. It was about his simple, audacious belief that he can make life better for others—even if all he had was a dream by a dusty stream.

From the neutralization of the terrifying polio that paralyzed President Franklin D. Roosevelt to the positive counterattack against the negative reception of Ebola in sub-Saharan Africa, from the malaria vaccine mandate designed to stop cerebral malaria from claiming lives, as it did with my brother Kingsley twelve years ago, to mitigating the asteroid strike of COVID-19, we have witnessed firsthand how powerful humanity can be when we choose to embrace it. Let it never be said that the right alliances and partnerships were not forged, and that we ignored the long awakening of a world once slumbering. Malcolm Gladwell might have framed it, to a worm in "horseradish, the world is horseradish"—a poignant reminder of how perspective can blind us to the larger truths around us.

Now, however, the global consciousness has stirred, challenging us to see beyond our confines and engage with the broader realities of change and accountability as the same forces are at play.

This should be the promised land—a place where abundance is not just an ideal but a reality. A coastline where milk and honey flow, symbolizing prosperity for those who work hard. Where clean, unrestricted water is a given, free speech is protected, and good jobs are within reach. It should be a land of universal healthcare, safe neighborhoods, and leadership that is both responsible and visionary, looking toward a brighter, more equitable future.

The reelections of President John D. Mahama of Ghana and particularly President Donald J. Trump, following his landslide victory and his return to the White House on January 20, 2025, alongside JD Vance and his avengers, has been widely seen as a triumph over "wokeism" and a reaffirmation of soundness within the body of Christ, as well as civility and eternal purpose. It is mandated by the people and poised to be a signal of a renewed sense of direction, a prosecutor that we can still find our way when we are guided by clarity and conviction.

The future Vice President's safari—from being born to a drug-addicted mother in a forgotten part of his country, serving in the Marine Corps, deploying overseas, utilizing the GI Bill to attend college, graduating from Yale Law School and on his way to become the third youngest Vice President of the United States— is a testament to resilience and the promise of opportunity.

Everywhere I look, there remains work to be done, and Pastor Julius Addi not only understands this but embodies it. A devoted family man, his life reflects unwavering loyalty, relentless hard work, and a deep commitment to fellowship. His extraordinary journey includes distinguished service in the British Royal Army, where he displayed remarkable courage, even surviving a gunshot wound to the chest during his deployment in Afghanistan's unforgiving terrain. With a strong foundation in business accounting and software, the servant of God could have chosen a conventional path, focusing solely on his family. Instead, nearly a decade ago, he founded and continues to lead Life and Spirit Arena, housed in the iconic C7 Church building in Glasgow. His mission is clear: to shape lives and empower the community, fostering meaningful, positive change in the everyday fabric of society.

This story serves as a powerful notification of the transformative power of faith and service, offering hope to those facing their own struggles. This stands in stark contrast to the likes of Boris Johnson, who, instead of offering constructive leadership, blamed the Church of England for the obesity crisis, suggesting that its failure to provide spiritual nourishment led people to overindulge. A misguided view, especially when we consider the true challenges of modern life, rather than placing blame on institutions. This example proves that no matter the challenges, purpose and dedication can lead to extraordinary things even in small credence.

From my couch to the ceremonial velvet red carpets of the regions of the world, countries could emulate the constructive strategy to make motherhood attractive again. Hungary is an exceptional case of a country that has effectively put family-centered policies into practice, and the results have been evident. From the moment Prime Minister Viktor Orbán took office in 2010, and was motorcaded to Sándor Palota neoclassical building situated in the Buda Castle

District in Budapest, his government has rolled out major reforms to encourage higher birth rates among married couples. These measures include generous tax breaks, assistance with home down payments, and exemptions for women who have at least four children.

President Nayib Bukele of El Salvador has swiftly redefined his country's economic trajectory, earning high marks in Moody's ratings for his government's handling of fiscal policy and long-term currency stability. Since his unprecedented rise to power, Bukele has made remarkable strides in reshaping the nation's future. Under his leadership, El Salvador has not only opened its doors to greater economic opportunity but also secured a prominent seat at the global table, much like Mephibosheth, who was welcomed to dine at King David's side. Today, his leadership has become a model for others, with foreign leaders coming to El Salvador to learn from his innovative approach and bolder reforms laid for his people.

Whenever ideological conflicts erupted on Earth, the International Space Station (ISS), no matter how increasingly complex their work station became never abandoned their posts. This is an act of peaceful ambassadorial duties of international cooperation. The astronauts aboard the ISS are generally not equipped to intervene in geopolitical issues. Their focalization is centered on scientific discovery and watchman's technological acumen for the safety and integrity of the planet earth. They may go as Russians, Chinese, Americans or Africans but, they reside in a collective containment as a unit, fulfills their fair shares, despite the turmoil on the planet. This dedication to uphold a neutral ground regardless of nationality, and continues their constitutional mandates over trivial logistical matter is worth mentioning and replication.

President Vladamir Putin may be whomever you want your opinions or fact-findings to be, however this is a leader who is willing to sit down even with the most contentious players on the global stage, including the Taliban, in pursuit of what he sees as constructive reform and strategic dialogue as well as takes precedence, aiming to curb violence on Moscow's streets and enforces his government's strict interpretation of cultural norms, and a land free from Sodom and Gomorrah.

The spirit of humanity—the breath of life and vitality within the people—must be cultivated, not forsaken. History has shown that in moments of moral and societal decline, majorities have empowered destructive leaders like Adolf Hitler, Idi Amin, or Ruto, with catastrophic outcomes.

Although, I choose to believe that beneath the surface of even the most fractured societies lies a reservoir of goodness. It is this inherent decency within the human heart, though often obscured, that holds the potential to compartmentalize us toward redemption and renewal.

I choose to believe that the significance of the essay, that a young Martin Luther King Junior wrote when he was seated in a prison cell as it is choreographed in the first book of Corinthians three and nine; "that humans progress does not roll on the wheels of inevitability; it comes through the timeless efforts of men willing to be coworkers with God." is still universality vital and not dead.

I choose to believe that all men are called to fatherhood. For most this will take a form of parenthood. A much smaller subset of men will become spiritual fathers through a religious vocation like - Evangelist Eric and Prophet Felix – my two big brothers. But to reject this call entirely and live only for yourself is to remain stuck in the trenches and in a perpetual state of emotional and psychological adolescence.

As I conclude work on this book, news of a ceasefire between Israel and Hezbollah regarding the conflict in Lebanon offers a rare glimmer of hope in an otherwise bleak narrative. The efforts of the administrations involved deserve acknowledgment for brokering this agreement. However, one cannot ignore the uncomfortable reality: these are the same actors who permitted the violence to escalate unchecked, raising the inevitable question—why was decisive action not taken sooner to prevent such devastating loss of life? Nevertheless, this truce represents a pivotal opportunity. It offers Israel a safeguard against further tragedies like those of October 7th and grants Lebanon a desperately needed respite from ongoing strife. The challenge now may lie in extending this momentum to Gaza.

Achieving a parallel suspension of hostilities there would signal not just a pause in bloodshed but a meaningful shift toward prioritizing diplomacy and sustainable peace over the entrenched cycles of violence that have defined the region for far too long. It's time to lift this cloud for good and create a new era of dialogue, perspectives, trust and peace. Let the future say of our generation that we sent forth mighty torrents of hope, decency, and that we worked together to heal and safeguard this world. Though we remain mere mortals, we are wiser, more intelligent, and better equipped —regardless of our size or scale—than the primitive eras of the past.

The United Nations must come to the speedily realization of its rightful place and the righteous position of which it was manufactured in the first place which was, and *should always be* to end wars and not to cherry-pick the sides of those with big infrastructural components and oil fields and tanks full of uranium enrichment compounds and hidden truths and treasures. The freedom fighters should give the people hope and not take it away from them with brutality and fatality.

The Pope, priests, and preachers must rise from their donjons and deadened routines, stepping into a new path of reclamation and restoration for the people through Christ Jesus.

This journey should not only inspire spiritual renewal but also empower individuals with a sense of purpose—much like the disciplined practice of Jiu Jitsu, which teaches strength, focus, and resilience. It is time for faith leaders to lead boldly, guiding their congregations toward a revitalized sense of hope and action that transcends mere words and becomes a living, transformative force. In the timelessness of God, future generations are as vital as our own, and it is our duty to act swiftly and resolutely—through every possible means—to unite humanity. This includes not only creating avenues for healing, but also ensuring that those who have erred are given the opportunity to reintegrate into society as responsible, productive members.

President Emmanuel Macron has done a wonderful job ensuring the full restoration and resurrection of the magnificent and historic Notre Dame Cathedral after a devasting fire five years ago. This is our solemn obligation. We are bound together by more than just charm, charisma, and chutzpah; we are connected by the technological habits and shared responsibilities that shape our collective existence.

Investments into high-speed marvel trains capable of reaching 1000km/h aimed to outpace airplanes using magnetic levitation in near-vacuum tubes, 5G powered for seamless communication, do not only showcase China's leap in transportation technology, but indicates that humanity is capable for greater innovation when there is peace.

No matter how unfathomable the circumstances may seem; this is our world. Something monumental is not just anticipated—it is imperative.

As we stand at the threshold of an unknown 2025, this decade is not reserved solely for the likes of tech moguls such as Elon Musk and his enduring Mars revolutionary vision or the highly anticipated second term Trump Administration of the United States of America or the hopes of the Reform party in the United Kingdom to win the 2029 general election or the village boy with a city dream like Victor Carson.

Above all, it belongs particularly to the young generation and those who are young in heart — different cohorts on the precipice of reshaping the future. The instance has come to march forward and remodulate the formal courses and chart the uncharted terrain, one that redefines the possibilities of what lies ahead. Let us walk together, with courage and distinction but with greater urgency and purpose, advancing further and - Niagara Falls - faster. This time, let us carry banners of hope and victory, emblazoned with the affirmation, "We have faced this before, we have stood here before, and we will triumph again."

From the balcony of my childhood's home to the coruscating chambers of John Lewis within the hedge of Buchanan Galleries, and onward to the majestic and historic steps of Lincoln in Washinton, DC, I stand resolute, holding the line with determination. I will continue to don my deep navy-blue suit, savor my signature chai latte, and carry on with the rhythms of my daily work—serving both God and the people. Together with the people of Great Britain, I will lift my voice to sing *God Save the King*, while my thoughts wander to the indomitable *ubuntu* spirit of the Black people of Africa.

I will strive to honor the essence of Scotland's cushion and Nicola Sturgeon's camaraderie without letting the excerpts of "you-know-what-I-mean" or "urrmm" or "wee" or "mate" to slip into my speeches by being articulated.

I will continue my conversations with Duchess, my most steadfast confidante and loyal audience, assured in the knowledge that; as John Lennon aptly put it, "You may say I'm a dreamer," but as this book goes to print, I came to a profound realization: "I am not the only one." And there is always a way out of the dungeons and dragons, but this time, just this time, I was the one to unlock the gate.

ACKNOWLEDGEMENTS

First and foremost, all glory to Christ the King – our Lord and Savior, the highest priesthood; for his ceaseless goodness and faithfulness throughout my life.

Secondly to the publishers for your boldness in printing this book.

Thirdly, to you, the reader - mostly writers forget about you - for not only choosing to engage with this book or recommending it to your friends, families and fireworks, but for taking action and getting to work after readership.

Last, but most definitely not least, is my cherished friend, MBD, who devoted herself to this journey, reading every word of my manuscript countless times, offering honest feedback—even when I was reluctant to hear it, supported me when I felt like allowing the swamp to devour me, and celebrated with me during times of progress. So much of the credit for both this book and the happy life I lead belongs to her.

ABOUT THE AUTHOR

© Maxwell Frimpong.

Victor Carson is a bestselling author, a Ghanaian-born and a resident of Great Britain. Victor is a first generation, stalwart to the ideas of community, faith and service. Victor is the founder and President of the PIWC Book Club (PBC) in Glasgow, Scotland, U.K, a dynamic platform for sharing ideas and engaging with literature. Victor is a principal member of the Climate Cardinals European Chapter.

Before that, he co-foundered and preceded as the President of Youth Focus Organization in Africa. Victor is the Chief Administrator of Life and Spirit Arena, Glasgow, Scotland, U.K, where he serves as the intermediary between relevant stakeholders and the faithful members, and supports their personal and reformational growth. Victor is an eternal optimist, lifelong learner, welcomes entrepreneurship, constructive diplomacy and golf courses.

COPYRIGHT

Amazon.

Printed in Great Britain
by Amazon

62035922R00201